Taking An ASE Certification Test

This study guide will help prepare you to take the ASE test. It contains descriptions of the types of questions used on the test, the task list from which the test questions are derived, a review of the task list subject information, and a practice test containing ASE style questions.

ABOUT ASE

The National Institute for Automotive Service Excellence (ASE) is a non-profit organization founded in 1972 for the purpose of improving the quality of automotive service and repair through the voluntary testing and certification of automotive technicians. Currently, there are over 400,000 professional technicians certified by ASE in over 40 different specialist areas.

ASE certification recognizes your knowledge and experience, and since it is voluntary, taking and passing an ASE certification test also demonstrates to employ-

ers and customers your commitment to your profession. It can mean better compensation and increased employment opportunities as well.

ASE not only certifies technician competency, it also promotes the benefits of technician certification to the motoring public. Repair shops that employ at least one ASE technician can display the ASE sign. Establishments where 75% of technicians are certified, with at least one technician certified in each area of service offered by the business, are eligible for the ASE Blue Seal of Excellence program. ASE encourages consumers to patronize these shops through media campaigns and car care clinics.

To become ASE certified, you must pass at least one ASE exam and have at least two years of related work experience. Technicians that pass all tests in a series earn Master Technician

status. Your certification is valid for five years, after which time you must retest to retain certification, demonstrating that you have kept up with the changing technology in the field.

THE ASE TEST

An ASE test consists of forty to eighty multiple-choice questions. Test questions are written by a panel of technical experts from vehicle, parts and equipment manufacturers, as well as working technicians and technical education instructors. All questions have been pre-tested and quality checked on a national sample of technicians. The questions are derived from information presented in the task list, which details the knowledge that a technician must have to pass an ASE test and be recognized as competent in that category. The task list is periodically updated by ASE in response to changes in vehicle technology and repair techniques.

Customer Service 1-800-240-1968
FAX 218-740-6417
e-mail www.ma@superfill.com
URL: www.motorage.com
A3 - MANUAL DRIVETRAIN AND AXLES

Taking An ASE Certification Test

There are five types of questions on an ASE test:

Direct, or Completion
MOST Likely
Technician A and Technician B
EXCEPT
LEAST Likely

Direct, or Completion

This type of question is the kind that is most familiar to anyone who has taken a multiple-choice test: you must answer a direct question or complete a statement with the correct answer. There are four choices given as potential answers, but only one is correct. Sometimes the correct answer to one of these questions is clear, however in other cases more than one answer may seem to be correct. In that case, read the question carefully and choose the answer that is most correct. Here is an example of this type of test question:

A compression test shows that one cylinder is too low. A leakage test on that cylinder shows that there is excessive leakage. During the test, air could be heard coming from the tailpipe. Which of the following could be the cause?

    A. broken piston rings
    B. bad head gasket
    C. bad exhaust gasket
    D. an exhaust valve not seating

There is only one correct answer to this question, answer D. If an exhaust valve is not seated, air will leak from the combustion chamber by way of the valve out to the tailpipe and make an audible sound. Answer C is wrong because an exhaust gasket has nothing to do with combustion chamber sealing. Answers A and B are wrong because broken rings or a bad head gasket would have air leaking through the oil filler or coolant system.

MOST Likely

This type of question is similar to a direct question but it can be more challenging because all or some of the answers may be nearly correct. However, only one answer is the most correct. For example:

When a cylinder head with an overhead camshaft is discovered to be warped, which of the following is the **MOST** correct repair option?

    A. replace the head
    B. check for cracks, straighten the head, surface the head
    C. surface the head, then straighten it
    D. straighten the head, surface the head, check for cracks

The most correct answer is B. It makes no sense to perform repairs on a cylinder head that might not be useable. The head should first be checked for warpage and cracks. Therefore, answer B is more correct than answer D. The head could certainly be replaced, but the cost factor may be prohibitive and availability may be limited, so answer B is more correct than answer A. If the top of the head is warped enough to interfere with cam bore alignment and/or restrict free movement of the camshaft, the head must be straightened before it is resurfaced, so answer C is wrong.

Technician A and Technician B

These questions are the kind most commonly associated with the ASE test. With these questions you are asked to choose which technician statement is correct, or whether they both are correct or incorrect. This type of question can be difficult because very often you may find one technician's statement to be clearly correct or incorrect while the other may not be so obvious. Do you choose one technician or both? The key to answering these questions is to carefully examine each technician's statement independently and judge it on its own merit. Here is an example of this type of question.

A vehicle equipped with rack-and-pinion steering is having the front end inspected. Technician A says that the inner tie-rod ends should be inspected while in their normal running position. Technician B says that if movement is felt between the tie-rod stud and the socket while the tire is moved in and out, the inner tie-rod should be replaced. Who is correct?

    A. Technician A only
    B. Technician B only
    C. Both A and B
    D. Neither A or B

The correct answer is C; both technicians' statements are correct. Technician B is clearly correct because any play felt between the tie-rod stud and the socket while the tire is moved in and out indicates that the assembly is worn and requires replacement. However, Technician A is also correct because inner tie-rods should be inspected while in their normal running position, to prevent binding that may occur when the suspension is allowed to hang free.

EXCEPT

This kind of question is sometimes called a negative question because you are asked to give the incorrect answer. All of the possible answers given are correct EXCEPT one. In effect, the correct answer to the question is the one that is wrong. The word EXCEPT is always capitalized in these questions. For example:

All of the following are true of torsion bars **EXCEPT:**
- A. They can be mounted longitudinally or transversely.
- B. They serve the same function as coil springs.
- C. They are interchangeable from side-to-side.
- D. They can be used to adjust vehicle ride height.

The correct answer is C. Torsion bars are not normally interchangeable from side-to-side. This is because the direction of the twisting or torsion is not the same on the left and right sides. All of the other answers contain true statements regarding torsion bars.

LEAST Likely

This type of question is similar to EXCEPT in that once again you are asked to give the answer that is wrong. For example:

Blue-gray smoke comes from the exhaust of a vehicle during deceleration. Of the following, which cause is **LEAST** likely?
- A. worn valve guides
- B. broken valve seals
- C. worn piston rings
- D. clogged oil return passages

The correct answer is C. Worn piston rings will usually make an engine smoke worse under acceleration. All of the other causes can allow oil to be drawn through the valve guides

under the high intake vacuum that occurs during deceleration.

PREPARING FOR THE ASE TEST

Begin preparing for the test by reading the task list. The task list describes the actual work performed by a technician in a particular specialty area. Each question on an ASE test is derived from a task or set of tasks in the list. Familiarizing yourself with the task list will help you to concentrate on the areas where you need to study.

The text section of this study guide contains information pertaining to each of the tasks in the task list. Reviewing this information will prepare you to take the practice test.

Take the practice test and compare your answers with the correct answer explanations. If you get an answer wrong and don't understand why, go back and read the information pertaining to that question in the text.

After reviewing the tasks and the subject information and taking the practice test, you should be prepared to take the ASE test or be aware of areas where further study is needed. When studying with this study guide or any other source of information, use the following guidelines to make sure the time spent is as productive as possible:

• Concentrate on the subject areas where you are weakest.
• Arrange your schedule to allow specific times for studying.
• Study in an area where you will not be distracted.
• Don't try to study after a full meal or when you are tired.
• Don't wait until the last minute and try to 'cram' for the test.

TAKING THE ASE TEST

Make sure you get a good night's sleep the night before the test. Have a good lunch on test day but either eat lightly or skip dinner until after the test. A heavy meal will make you tired.

Bring your admission ticket, some form of photo identification, three or four sharpened #2 pencils and a watch (to keep track of time as the test room may not have a clock) with you to the test center.

The test proctor will explain how to fill out the answer sheet and how much time is allotted for each test. You may take up to four certification tests in one sitting, but this may prove too difficult unless you are very familiar with the subject areas.

When the test begins, open the test booklet to see how many questions are on the test. This will help you keep track of your progress against the time remaining. Mark your answer sheet clearly, making sure the answer number and question number correspond.

Read through each question carefully. If you don't know the answer to a question and need to think about it, move on to the next question. Don't spend too much time on any one question. After you have worked through to the end of the test, check your remaining time and go back and answer the questions you had trouble with. Very often, information found in questions later in the test can help answer some of the ones with which you had difficulty.

If you are running out of time and still have unanswered test questions, guess the answers if necessary to make sure every question is answered. Do not leave any answers blank. It is to your advantage to answer every question, because your test score is based on the number of correct answers. A guessed answer could be correct, but a blank answer can never be.

To learn exactly where and when the ASE Certification Tests are available in your area, as well as the costs involved in becoming ASE certified, please contact ASE directly for a registration booklet.

The National Institute for Automotive Service Excellence
101 Blue Seal Drive, S.E.
Suite 101
Leesburg, VA 20175

1-877-ASE-TECH (273-8324)

http://www.asecert.org

TRAINING FOR CERTIFICATION

Table of Contents

A3 - Manual Drivetrain And Axles

Manual Drivetrain And Axles

TEST SPECIFICATIONS
FOR MANUAL DRIVETRAIN AND AXLES (TEST A3)

CONTENT AREA	NUMBER OF QUESTIONS IN ASE TEST	PERCENTAGE OF COVERAGE IN ASE TEST
A. Clutch Diagnosis And Repair	6	15%
B. Transmission Diagnosis And Repair	7	15%
C. Transaxle Diagnosis And Repair	8	20%
D. Driveshaft/Halfshaft And Universal Joint/Constant Velocity (CV) Joint Diagnosis And Repair (Front- And Rear-Wheel Drive)	5	15%
E. Rear Axle Diagnosis And Repair	7	17%
1. Ring And Pinion Gears (3)		
2. Differential Case/Carrier Assembly (2)		
3. Limited Slip/Locking Differential (1)		
4. Axle Shafts (1)		
F. Four-Wheel Drive/All-Wheel Drive Component Diagnosis And Repair	7	17%
Total	**40**	**100%**

The 5-year Recertification Test will cover the same content areas as those listed above. However, the number of questions in each content area of the Recertification Test will be reduced by about one-half.

The following pages list the tasks covered in each content area. These task descriptions offer detailed information to technicians preparing for the test, and to persons who may be instructing Manual Drivetrain And Axles technicians. The task list may also serve as a guideline for question writers, reviewers and test assemblers.

It should be noted that the number of questions in each content area may not equal the number of tasks listed. Some of the tasks are complex and broad in scope, and may be covered by several questions. Other tasks are simple and narrow in scope; one question may cover several tasks. The main purpose for listing the tasks is to describe accurately what is done on the job, not to make each task correspond to a particular test question.

MANUAL DRIVETRAIN AND AXLES TEST TASK LIST

A. CLUTCH DIAGNOSIS AND REPAIR
(6 questions)

Task 1 - Diagnose clutch noise, binding, slippage, pulsation, chatter, pedal feel/effort and release problems; determine needed repairs.

Task 2 - Inspect, adjust and replace clutch pedal linkage, cables and automatic adjuster mechanisms, brackets, bushings, pivots, springs and electrical switches.

Task 3 - Inspect, adjust, replace and bleed hydraulic clutch slave cylinder/actuator, master cylinder, lines and hoses; clean and flush hydraulic system; refill with proper fluid.

Task 4 - Inspect, adjust and replace release (throw-out) bearing, bearing retainer, lever and pivot.

Task 5 - Inspect and replace clutch disc and pressure plate assembly; inspect input shaft splines.

Task 6 - Inspect and replace pilot bearing/bushing; inspect pilot bearing/bushing mating surfaces.

Task 7 - Inspect and measure flywheel and ring gear; inspect dual-mass flywheel damper where required; repair or replace as necessary.

Task 8 - Inspect engine block, clutch (bell) housing, transmission case mating surfaces and alignment dowels; determine needed repairs.

Task 9 - Measure flywheel surface runout and crankshaft end-play; determine needed repairs.

Task 10 - Inspect, replace and align powertrain mounts.

B. TRANSMISSION DIAGNOSIS AND REPAIR
(7 questions)

Task 1 - Diagnose transmission noise, hard shifting, gear clash, jumping out of gear, fluid condition and type, and fluid leakage problems; determine needed repairs.

Task 2 - Inspect, adjust and replace transmission external shifter assembly, shift linkages, brackets, bushings/grommets, pivots and levers.

Task 3 - Inspect and replace transmission gaskets, sealants, seals and fasteners; inspect sealing surfaces.

Task 4 - Remove and replace transmission; inspect transmission mounts.

Task 5 - Disassemble and clean transmission components; reassemble transmission.

Task 6 - Inspect, repair and/or replace transmission shift cover and internal shift forks, bushings, bearings, levers, shafts, sleeves, detent mechanisms, interlocks and springs.

Task 7 - Inspect and replace input (clutch) shaft, bearings and retainers.

Task 8 - Inspect and replace mainshaft, gears, thrust washers, bearings and retainers/snaprings; measure gear clearance/end-play.

Task 9 - Inspect and replace synchronizer hub, sleeve, keys (inserts), springs and blocking (synchronizing) rings/mechanisms; measure blocking ring clearance.

Task 10 - Inspect and replace countershaft, counter (cluster) gear, bearings, thrust washers and retainers/snaprings.

Task 11 - Inspect and replace reverse idler gear, shaft, bearings, thrust washers and retainers/snaprings.

Task 12 - Measure and adjust shaft/gear and synchronizer end-play.

Task 13 - Measure and adjust bearing preload or end-play.

Task 14 - Inspect, repair and replace extension housing and transmission case mating surfaces, bores, bushings and vents.

Task 15 - Inspect and replace the speedometer drive gear, driven gear and retainers.

Task 16 - Inspect, test and replace transmission sensors and switches.

Task 17 - Inspect lubrication systems.

Task 18 - Check fluid level and refill with proper fluid.

C. TRANSAXLE DIAGNOSIS AND REPAIR
(8 questions)

Task 1 - Diagnose transaxle noise, hard shifting, gear clash, jumping out of gear, fluid condition and type, and fluid leakage problems; determine needed repairs.

Task 2 - Inspect, adjust, lubricate and replace transaxle external shift assemblies, linkages, brackets, bushings/grommets, cables, pivots and levers.

Task 3 - Inspect and replace transaxle gaskets, sealants, seals and fasteners; inspect sealing surfaces.

Task 4 - Remove and replace transaxle; inspect, replace and align transaxle mounts and subframe/cradle assembly.

Task 5 - Disassemble and clean transaxle components; reassemble transaxle.

Task 6 - Inspect, repair and/or replace transaxle shift cover and internal shift forks, levers, bushings, shafts, sleeves, detent mechanisms, interlocks and springs.

Task 7 - Inspect and replace input shaft, gears, bearings and retainers/snaprings.

Task 8 - Inspect and replace output shaft, gears, thrust washers, bearings and retainers/snaprings.

Task 9 - Inspect and replace synchronizer hub, sleeve, keys (inserts), springs and blocking (synchronizing) rings; measure blocking ring clearance.

Task 10 - Inspect and replace reverse idler gear, shaft, bearings, thrust washers and retainers/snaprings.

Task 11 - Inspect, repair and/or replace transaxle case mating surfaces, bores, dowels, bushings, bearings and vents.

Task 12 - Inspect and replace the speedometer drive gear, driven gear and retainers.

Task 13 - Inspect, test and replace transaxle sensors and switches.

Task 14 - Diagnose differential assembly noise and vibration problems; determine needed repairs.

Task 15 - Remove and replace differential final drive assembly.

Task 16 - Inspect, measure, adjust and replace differential pinion gears (spiders), shaft, side gears, thrust washers and case.

Task 17 - Inspect and replace differential side bearings; inspect case.

Task 18 - Measure shaft preload/end-play (shim/spacer selection procedure).

Task 19 - Inspect lubrication systems.

Task 20 - Check fluid level and refill with proper fluid.

Task 21 - Measure and adjust differential bearing preload/end-play.

D. DRIVESHAFT/HALFSHAFT AND UNIVERSAL JOINT/ CONSTANT VELOCITY (CV) JOINT DIAGNOSIS AND REPAIR (FRONT- AND REAR-WHEEL DRIVE)
(5 questions)

Task 1 - Diagnose shaft and universal/CV-joint noise and vibration problems; determine needed repairs.

Task 2 - Inspect, service and replace shafts, yokes, boots and universal/CV-joints; verify proper phasing.

Task 3 - Inspect, service and replace shaft center support bearings.

Task 4 - Check and correct drive/propeller shaft balance.

Task 5 - Measure driveshaft runout.

Task 6 - Measure and adjust driveshaft working angles.

Task 7 - Inspect, service and replace front wheel bearings, seals and hubs.

E. REAR-WHEEL DRIVE AXLE DIAGNOSIS AND REPAIR
(7 questions)

1. Ring And Pinion Gears
(3 questions)

Task 1 - Diagnose noise, vibration and fluid leakage problems; determine needed repairs.

Task 2 - Inspect and replace companion flange and pinion seal; measure companion flange runout.

Task 3 - Measure ring gear runout; determine needed repairs.

Task 4 - Inspect and replace ring and pinion gear set, collapsible spacers, sleeves (shims) and bearings.

Task 5 - Measure and adjust drive pinion depth.

Task 6 - Measure and adjust drive pinion bearing preload (collapsible spacer or shim type).

Task 7 - Measure and adjust differential (side) bearing preload and ring and pinion backlash (threaded adjuster or shim type).

Task 8 - Perform ring and pinion tooth contact pattern checks; determine needed adjustments.

2. Differential Case/Carrier Assembly
(2 questions)

Task 1 - Diagnose differential assembly noise and vibration problems; determine needed repairs.

Task 2 - Remove and replace differential assembly.

Task 3 - Inspect, measure, adjust and replace differential pinion gears (spiders), shaft, side gears, thrust washers and case/carrier.

Task 4 - Inspect and replace differential side bearings; inspect case/carrier.

Task 5 - Measure differential case/carrier runout; determine needed repairs.

Task 6 - Inspect axle housing and vent.

3. Limited Slip/Locking Differential
(1 question)

Task 1 - Diagnose limited slip differential noise, slippage and chatter problems; determine needed repairs.

Task 2 - Inspect, drain and refill with correct lubricant.

Task 3 - Inspect, adjust and replace clutch (cone/plate) pack or locking assembly.

4. Axle Shafts
(1 question)

Task 1 - Diagnose rear axle shaft noise, vibration and fluid leakage problems; determine needed repairs.

Task 2 - Inspect and replace rear axle shaft wheel studs.

Task 3 - Remove, inspect and/or replace rear axle shafts, splines, seals, bearings and retainers.

Task 4 - Measure rear axle flange runout and shaft end-play; determine needed repairs..

F. FOUR-WHEEL DRIVE/ALL-WHEEL DRIVE COMPONENT DIAGNOSIS AND REPAIR
(7 questions)

Task 1 - Diagnose drive assembly noise, vibration, shifting, leakage and steering problems; determine needed repairs.

Task 2 - Inspect, adjust and repair transfer case manual shifting mechanisms, bushings, mounts, levers and brackets.

Task 3 - Remove and replace transfer case.

Task 4 - Disassemble transfer case; clean and inspect internal transfer case components; determine needed repairs.

Task 5 - Reassemble transfer case; refill with proper fluid.

Task 6 - Check transfer case fluid level, condition and type.

Task 7 - Inspect, service and replace front drive/propeller shaft and universal/CV-joints.

Task 8 - Inspect, service and replace front drive axle universal/CV-joints and drive/halfshafts.

Task 9 - Inspect, service and replace front wheel bearings, seals and hubs.

Task 10 - Check transfer case and front axle seals and all vents.

Task 11 - Diagnose, test, adjust and replace electrical/electronic components of four-wheel/all-wheel drive systems.

Task 12 - Test, diagnose and replace axle actuation and engagement systems (including: viscous, hydraulic, magnetic and mechanical).

The preceding Task List details all of the related subject matter you are expected to know in order to sit for this ASE Certification Test. Your own years of experience in the professional automotive service repair trade also should provide you with added background.

Finally, a conscientious review of the material provided in this Training for ASE Certification unit should help you to be adequately prepared to take this test.

We employ technicians certified by the National Institute for
AUTOMOTIVE SERVICE EXCELLENCE
Let us show you their credentials

CLUTCH DIAGNOSIS AND REPAIR

DESCRIPTION AND OPERATION

The clutch allows the driver to engage and disengage the engine from the drivetrain on a manual transmission vehicle. The clutch assembly consists of the flywheel, pressure plate, clutch disc, release bearing (also known as the throwout bearing), pilot bearing or bushing, bell housing and clutch release mechanism.

The flywheel is usually made of cast iron and performs multiple functions: it helps to smooth the engine's power delivery, the teeth around its circumference provide an engagement for the starter, and it provides the mounting points for the pressure plate and friction surface for the clutch disc.

The pressure plate is mounted on the flywheel and is the driving member of the clutch assembly. Coil springs or a diaphragm spring exert pressure on the clutch disc, holding it against the flywheel.

The clutch disc is a round plate covered with a friction material and is the driven member of the clutch assembly. It is sandwiched in between the flywheel and pressure plate, and is splined to the transmission input shaft, the end of which is supported by a pilot bearing or bushing mounted in the end of the crankshaft or the center of the flywheel.

The release bearing, or throwout bearing, is usually a sealed ball or roller bearing unit. It rides on a sleeve over the transmission input shaft and acts on the pressure plate to disengage the clutch disc when the clutch release mechanism is applied.

The bell housing, or clutch housing, connects the engine to the transmission and encloses the clutch assembly. It also provides mounting points for part of the clutch release mechanism.

There are three types of clutch release mechanisms, mechanical, cable and hydraulic. A mechanical mechanism uses a system of shafts and levers to transfer the motion of the clutch pedal to the release bearing.

A cable mechanism uses a braided wire cable that is connected between the clutch pedal and the release lever. The cable is enclosed in a flexible housing that is attached to the firewall and the bell housing. When the clutch pedal is depressed, the cable is drawn through the housing, pulling the release lever. The release lever forces the release bearing against the pressure plate, disengaging the clutch.

A hydraulic mechanism uses a master cylinder and slave cylinder connected by a hydraulic fluid line. The master cylinder is connected to the clutch pedal and the slave cylinder is connected to the release bearing. When the clutch pedal is depressed, hydraulic fluid flows from the master cylinder through the hydraulic fluid line to the slave cylinder. Pressure in the system causes the slave cylinder to act on the release bearing, disengaging the clutch.

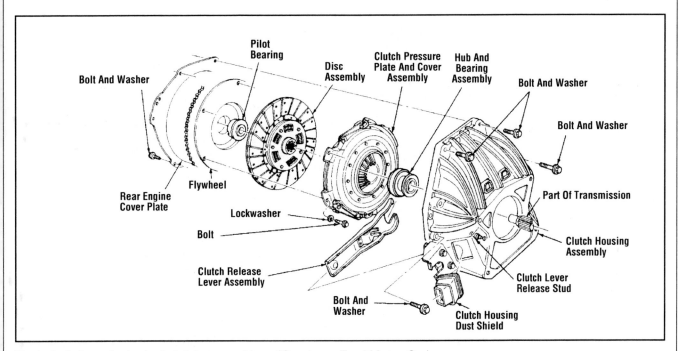

Exploded view of a typical clutch assembly.   *(Courtesy: Ford Motor Co.)*

When the clutch pedal is depressed, the clutch release mechanism forces the release bearing against the pressure plate fingers or diaphragm spring, pulling the pressure plate away from the clutch disc. The engine's crankshaft then turns without turning the clutch disc and transmission input shaft. When the clutch pedal is released, the release bearing is pulled away from the pressure plate and the pressure plate spring(s) force the clutch disc against the flywheel, locking the engine crankshaft and the transmission input shaft together.

DIAGNOSIS AND INSPECTION

Clutch failure can be caused by component wear, improper adjustment or driver abuse. Begin diagnosis by checking clutch pedal operation and driving the vehicle to check clutch performance.

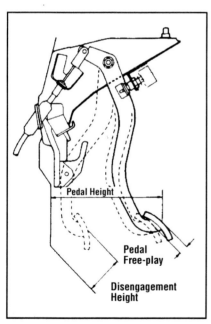

Pedal Height

Pedal Free-play

Disengagement Height

Common clutch pedal adjustment measuring points.

The clutch pedal should have the proper amount of free-play. Excessive free-play will not allow the clutch to disengage fully, and can cause difficulty and grinding noise when shifting the trans-

mission. Insufficient free-play can cause the clutch to be partially disengaged at all times. This can in turn cause premature release bearing wear and noise, pressure plate wear and clutch slippage. Refer to the vehicle service manual for clutch pedal height, free-play and travel specifications and adjustment procedures. Typically, mechanical linkage types are adjusted at the clutch release lever pushrod, cable systems are adjusted with an adjusting nut on the cable housing or are self-adjusting, and hydraulic systems are adjusted at the master cylinder and slave cylinder pushrods or are not adjustable.

Depress and release the clutch pedal with the engine off; the clutch should engage and disengage smoothly. If the pedal is stiff or binds, if the action is noisy, or if pedal adjustment to specification was not possible or has not corrected a problem, inspect the clutch pedal, bushings and linkage for wear, damage and lack of lubrication.

If the vehicle has hydraulic clutch linkage and the pedal is soft, there is excessive free-play or the clutch does not disengage when the pedal is depressed, it may be due to low fluid level in the master cylinder, worn seals or a leak in the hydraulic system. If the pedal is hard, it may be due to swollen seals in the master and/or slave cylinder caused by fluid contamination, a restricted hydraulic line or a blocked master cylinder compensating port. The compensating port can become blocked because of a binding master cylinder piston or by an incorrect master cylinder pushrod adjustment.

If the linkage looks OK, the problem is with the clutch assembly. The clutch disc hub may be binding on the input shaft splines. A scored or dry transmission bearing retainer could cause the release bearing to bind or make noise. The pressure plate fingers may be binding or broken, cocking the release

bearing. If the clutch pedal does not return from the floor, the pressure plate springs are probably fatigued. Removal of the clutch assembly will be required for further inspection.

Start the engine and operate the clutch pedal with the transmission in neutral and the parking brake applied. If a pulsation is felt through the pedal when light pressure is applied, suspect a warped flywheel, bent pressure plate fingers or a misaligned bell housing. A worn release bearing could cause a grinding noise when the clutch pedal is depressed.

Depress the clutch pedal and shift the transmission from first to second gear several times, and then shift into reverse gear. If the transmission makes a grinding noise when going into gear, the clutch is dragging and not releasing properly. Make sure that the clutch pedal free-play is adjusted correctly as excessive free-play is the most common cause for a dragging clutch. Worn bushings, bent linkage rods and elongated linkage rod holes can also contribute to insufficient release bearing travel. If equipped with a hydraulic clutch, check for leaks and air in the system. If the clutch release mechanism checks out OK, the problem is inside the bell housing and could be excessive crankshaft end-play, a warped clutch disc or pressure plate, or the clutch disc hub binding on the input shaft splines. Clutch drag can also be caused by a seized or binding pilot bushing or bearing.

A slipping clutch is usually indicated by an increase in engine speed without a corresponding increase in vehicle speed; the engine races when the vehicle is accelerated. To check for clutch slippage, apply the parking brake and place the transmission in high gear, then increase engine speed slightly and slowly release the clutch pedal. The engine should stall immediately if the clutch is in good condition. A partially slipping clutch will let the engine run momentarily without stalling while a badly slipping clutch may let the engine run even with the clutch fully released. Clutch slippage can be caused by insufficient clutch free-play, a worn clutch disc, weak pressure plate springs or oil on the friction surfaces. Insufficient free-play causes the release bearing to apply pressure to the pressure plate while in the released position, which can not only cause the clutch to slip but can also result in a worn out release bearing, clutch disc and pressure plate. As for the worn clutch disc, as the friction lining becomes thinner, the pressure plate will not be able to exert as much spring pressure and clamping force on the disc, causing clutch slippage.

There are a number of possible causes that can make the clutch grab or chatter as it is engaged. Among these are a bent, burned or glazed clutch disc, broken or weak torsional springs on the clutch disc, glazed or scored flywheel and pressure plate, worn input shaft splines, binding linkage and broken engine mounts. However, the most common cause is fluid contaminated friction surfaces. Fluid contamination can be from oil, caused by a leaking engine rear main seal or transmission input shaft seal, or from hydraulic fluid from a leaking clutch slave cylinder or hydraulic line.

CLUTCH SERVICE

Clutch Linkage

Mechanical Linkage

This system usually consists of two pushrods attached to levers on each end of a cross-shaft. The cross-shaft pivots on ball studs mounted on the frame and engine or bell housing. The other ends of the pushrods are connected to the clutch pedal and clutch release lever, respectively. The clutch release lever pivots on a shaft or ball stud and moves

the release bearing. There are also return springs to pull the release bearing away from the pressure plate and there are usually rubber or nylon bushings at the pivot points.

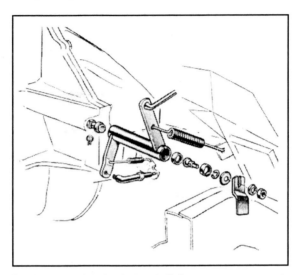

Typical mechanical clutch linkage arrangement. *(Courtesy: GM Corp.)*

Check the linkage for obvious damage like cracked, broken or bent rods and broken, stretched or missing return springs. Have an assistant slowly depress and release the clutch pedal while you watch the movement of the linkage. Look for signs of abnormal movement or a rod or lever moving significantly before its corresponding component moves, which would indicate wear in the pivot.

Use new clips or cotter pins when replacing linkage components, as required. If a bushing is worn or missing and the link is grooved from wear or the pivot hole is elongated, don't just install a new bushing, replace the worn part as well as the bushing. Lubricate linkage pivot points as required, and properly adjust the linkage once component replacement is completed. Adjustment of mechanical linkage is usually performed at the clutch fork pushrod; consult the vehicle service manual for the proper procedure and specification.

Cable Linkage

Clutch cables should follow a smooth arc from the clutch pedal to the release fork and clear all other components. Frayed, kinked or otherwise damaged cables should be replaced. Although it is unlikely, if the cable has been stretched, it must be replaced if proper adjustment is not possible.

Many cable systems are adjustable at their lower end where the cable attaches to the lower support bracket, usually on the bell housing. Others are adjustable from where the cable passes through the firewall. Usually this involves loosening the jam nut and changing the effective length of the cable by turning the adjuster nut, and then tightening the jam nut. Consult the vehicle service manual for the exact procedure and specification.

Many vehicles are equipped with a self-adjusting clutch, which removes play from the cable as components wear. To maintain the cable adjustment, a spring-loaded quadrant gear—attached to the clutch pedal shaft—rotates with the shaft and maintains proper cable length. As the clutch wears, the quadrant may no longer be able to maintain proper adjustment. A pawl engages a new tooth on the quadrant gear, taking up any slack in the cable. If the self-adjusting mechanism fails, the clutch will slip and wear prematurely. Make sure all the springs in the quadrant and pawl are intact and that the quadrant moves freely.

Replacing a conventionally adjusted clutch cable usually involves disconnecting the cable ends from the clutch pedal and release fork and disconnecting the cable housing from the

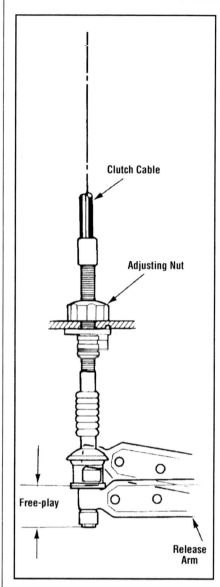

Typical cable adjustment location.
(Courtesy: Honda Motor Co.)

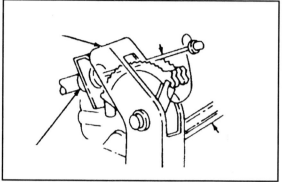

Cable installation on a self-adjusting mechanism.
(Courtesy: Ford Motor Co.)

Route the replacement cable through the firewall and into position. With the clutch pedal lifted up to release the pawl, rotate the gear quadrant forward and hook the cable into the gear quadrant. Prop up the clutch in the uppermost position, and then connect the other end of the cable to the bell housing and clutch release lever. Remove the clutch pedal prop and then adjust the clutch by depressing the pedal several times.

Hydraulic Linkage

Hydraulic clutch linkages operate much like hydraulic brake systems and the hydraulic fluid used in most systems is brake fluid. When the clutch pedal is depressed, it actuates a pushrod and piston in the clutch master cylinder, forcing fluid to act on the piston and pushrod of the slave cylinder. The slave cylinder's pushrod then actuates the release lever. If the master cylinder or slave cylinder fails, or if the hydraulic line ruptures, the clutch will stay engaged.

Check the fluid level in the master cylinder reservoir and inspect the fluid for moisture, dirt or contamination. Fluid that is mostly clear is in good condition. Fluid that appears cloudy contains a large amount of moisture. Dirty fluid will be dark in color.

If brake fluid is contaminated by petroleum or mineral based fluids, the rubber components in the hydraulic system will swell, possibly causing binding in the

mounting brackets at the firewall and bell housing. The new cable is then properly routed, connected and adjusted.

To replace a cable on a vehicle with a self-adjusting mechanism, prop up the clutch pedal to release the pawl from the quadrant. Disconnect the clutch cable from the release lever and cable housing from the bell housing. With the clutch pedal lifted up to release the pawl, rotate the gear quadrant forward and unhook the cable from the quadrant. Remove the cable through the firewall.

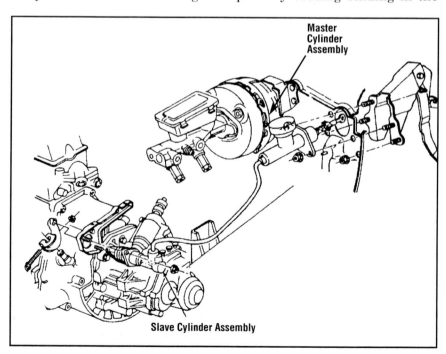

Typical hydraulic clutch actuating system.
(Courtesy: GM Corp.)

master and slave cylinders and a hard pedal. One way to tell if the fluid is contaminated is to put a spoonful of brake fluid from the master cylinder into a styrofoam cup filled with water. DOT 3 and DOT 4 fluid will completely dissolve in the water in a white cloud and then turn clear. Petroleum or mineral based fluids will float on the water's surface and dissolve the Styrofoam cup at the water line.

Contaminated brake fluid must be drained and flushed from the system. All rubber components must then be replaced and the system filled and bled using fresh brake fluid.

Inspect the hydraulic clutch system for fluid leaks at the hydraulic line and behind the master cylinder and slave cylinder dust boots. If there are no external leaks and there is a clutch problem due to insufficient travel of the release bearing, try bleeding air from the system. If there is no air in the system, and adjustment (if possible) is correct, and the release bearing does not move when the clutch pedal is depressed, there is an internal sealing problem and the master cylinder and/or slave cylinder must be replaced.

There are a variety of hydraulic clutch system designs. On some systems the master cylinder, slave cylinder and hydraulic fluid line can be replaced separately, while on others these components cannot be separated and must be replaced as a unit. Some vehicles have an internal slave cylinder and release bearing. Since this type of slave cylinder can only be replaced by removing the transmission, it is advisable to replace it whenever the clutch assembly is serviced.

When replacing any hydraulic part, it is important to bleed any air from the system. Some slave cylinders have bleeder screws and these are bled just like a brake hydraulic system. Connect a hose to the bleeder and submerge the other end in a clear container partially filled with

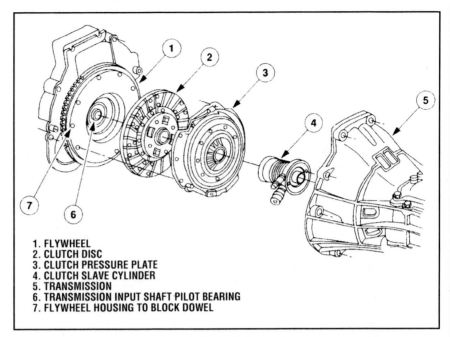

1. FLYWHEEL
2. CLUTCH DISC
3. CLUTCH PRESSURE PLATE
4. CLUTCH SLAVE CYLINDER
5. TRANSMISSION
6. TRANSMISSION INPUT SHAFT PILOT BEARING
7. FLYWHEEL HOUSING TO BLOCK DOWEL

A clutch with an internal slave cylinder/release bearing assembly. *(Courtesy: Ford Motor Co.)*

brake fluid. Make sure the master cylinder is filled. Have an assistant push down on the clutch pedal and then open the bleeder screw. When the pedal reaches the stop, tighten the bleeder screw and then have the assistant release the pedal. Repeat the process until no air bubbles are seen in the container.

On systems without bleeder screws, it may be necessary to remove the slave cylinder and cycle the slave cylinder pushrod in-and-out until no air bubbles are seen in the master cylinder reservoir. On other systems it may only be necessary to cycle the clutch pedal repeatedly until the air works its way up the system and into the master cylinder reservoir. On systems with a separate master cylinder, bench bleeding the master cylinder prior to installation helps speed up the bleeding process.

Hydraulic clutch systems are similar to disc brake hydraulic systems in that they are self-adjusting. However, on some vehicles an adjustment can be made, most often by turning a nut on the slave cylinder

pushrod. Consult the vehicle service manual for the correct procedure.

Clutch Switches

There are two electrical switches activated by the clutch pedal. The start/clutch interlock switch is a safety device that prevents the engine from starting with the transmission in gear. It prevents the starter from operating unless the clutch pedal is depressed. The other switch disengages the cruise control when the clutch pedal is depressed.

The start/clutch interlock switch is open when the clutch pedal is in the released position, interrupting current flow in the starter circuit. When the clutch pedal is depressed, the switch closes, allowing current flow in the circuit. If the starter engages with the clutch pedal released or if it does not engage with the pedal depressed, first check the switch adjustment. Refer to the service manual for specifications.

If adjustment is correct, check for voltage to the input side of the switch. If voltage is present at the input side, there should be no voltage at the output side of the switch when it is in the open position (pedal released), but there should be voltage at the output side when the switch is closed (pedal depressed). Replace the switch if it does not perform as specified.

The cruise control switch provides an input to the cruise control module assembly. However, the switch can operate differently depending on system configuration. On some vehicles, the cruise control switch is open when the clutch pedal is in the released position. When the clutch pedal is depressed, the cruise control switch closes, and voltage is supplied to the cruise control module, signaling the module to disengage the cruise control. On other vehicles, the switch is closed when the clutch pedal is released, completing the cruise control circuit, and open when the clutch pedal is depressed, interrupting the circuit and disengaging the cruise control. The cruise control switch can be tested in the same manner as the start/clutch interlock switch, but refer to the service manual for specific voltage/switch position specifications.

Clutch Assembly

Removal

Disconnect the clutch linkage from the bell housing. Remove the transmission or transaxle to gain access to the clutch assembly. On some vehicles the engine and transmission are removed as a unit and then separated; consult the vehicle service manual for the proper procedure. If the bell housing is not integral with the transmission, remove the bell housing from the engine block.

Examine the flywheel and pressure plate for locating dowels and alignment marks. If none are present and there is a chance that the pressure plate will be reused, paint or stamp alignment marks so the pressure plate can be reinstalled in the same location, in order to maintain balance. Install a clutch alignment

tool or old transmission input shaft into the pilot bushing or bearing, to keep the clutch disc and pressure plate from falling. Loosen the pressure plate bolts gradually and evenly, working in a criss-cross pattern. Hold the pressure plate against the flywheel as you remove the bolts, then remove the alignment tool, pressure plate and clutch disc from the flywheel.

Component Inspection

Inspect the pressure plate friction surface for cracks, scoring, heat checks and hard spots. Use a straightedge and feeler gauge to check the surface for warpage. Check the diaphragm spring or release fingers for bending, breakage and other wear. All of the release fingers or diaphragm spring must be at the same level. Replace the pressure plate if any defects are found.

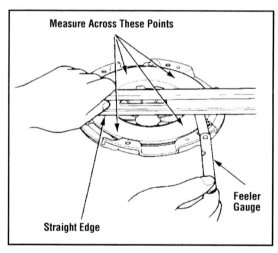

Measure Across These Points

Straight Edge

Feeler Gauge

Checking the clutch pressure plate friction surface for warpage.
(Courtesy: Honda Motor Co.)

Inspect the clutch disc friction surface for wear, damage and evidence of oil contamination. Measure the overall disc thickness and the thickness of the lining above the rivets, and compare with specifications. Inspect the torsion springs for breakage and looseness. Check the clutch disc hub splines for excessive wear. Check the splines on the

transmission input shaft for rust, burrs or other wear. Slide the disc onto the transmission input shaft and check for looseness or binding. If the input shaft splines are worn, damaged or twisted, the transmission must be disassembled and the input shaft replaced. With the clutch disc installed on the input shaft, or using a suitable fixture, rotate the clutch disc and check the runout using a dial indicator; compare with specification. Unless the disc is undamaged and has very little wear, it should be replaced.

Examine the release bearing, or throwout bearing, for obvious damage. Rotate the bearing while applying pressure to the clutch finger contact surface; it should turn smoothly with no roughness. Check the release bearing contact surface of the transmission bearing retainer for wear and replace as necessary. It is a good practice to replace the release bearing whenever the clutch is serviced.

Inspect the release lever, or clutch fork for wear and damage. Check the ends that contact the release bearing and pushrod as well as the pivot. Replace the fork/lever and the pivot if they are worn or damaged.

Inspect the flywheel surface for cracks, scoring, heat checks and hard spots. Check flywheel runout using a dial indicator and compare with specification. To ensure an accurate reading, push in on the flywheel as it is turned to take up the crankshaft thrust bearing clearance. While the dial indicator is in place, measure the crankshaft thrust bearing clearance. Push the flywheel forward against the thrust bearing, zero the dial indicator, and then pry evenly on both sides of the flywheel to pull it back. If the flywheel surface is worn or there is excessive runout,

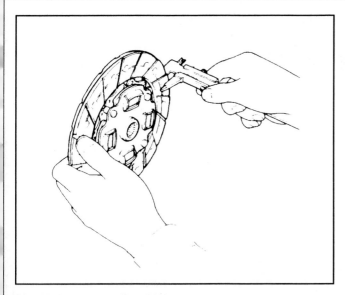

Measuring clutch disc thickness.
(Courtesy: Honda Motor Co.)

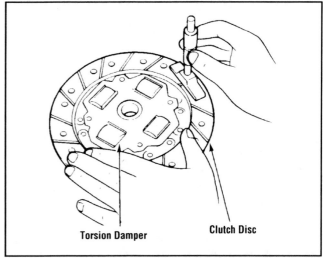

Torsion Damper   **Clutch Disc**

Measuring clutch disc lining thickness above the rivet head.
(Courtesy: Honda Motor Co.)

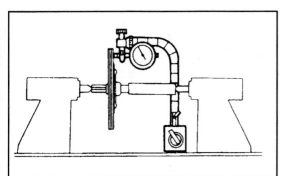

Measuring clutch disc runout.
(Courtesy: Ford Motor Co.)

the flywheel should be resurfaced. In cases of extreme wear or damage, replacement may be necessary. If crank-shaft thrust bearing clearance is excessive, the thrust bearing and possibly the crankshaft will require replacement.

Check the flywheel ring gear for worn, chipped or missing teeth. Ring gear replacement is possible on some flywheels, but on others, replacement of the entire flywheel is necessary if ring gear teeth are damaged. Before removing the flywheel from the crankshaft for resurfacing or replacement, mark its position on the crankshaft so balance will be maintained at installation.

Examine the pilot bearing or bushing for wear or damage. Rotate bearings and check for roughness and binding. Check bushings for wear, burning and scoring. Measure the bushing inside diameter and compare with specification. The pilot bushing/bearing can be located in the crankshaft or flywheel. If replacement is necessary, remove the pilot bushing/bearing from a flywheel using a suitable driver. Bearings/bushings can be removed from the

Dial Indicator

Measuring flywheel runout.
(Courtesy: Honda Motor Co.)

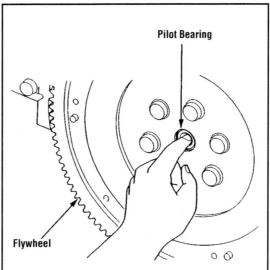

Pilot Bearing

Flywheel

Inspecting the pilot bearing.
(Courtesy: Honda Motor Co.)

crankshaft using a slide hammer or puller. As an alternative method of bushing removal, fill the cavity in the crankshaft behind the bushing with grease, then insert an input shaft or clutch alignment tool into the bushing and tap with a mallet, using hydraulic pressure to remove the bushing.

Finally, if there was evidence of oil contamination on clutch components or a buildup of oil

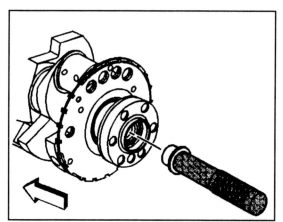

Removing the pilot bearing from the crankshaft using a puller. *(Courtesy: GM Corp.)*

residue on the back of the engine block or bell housing, the rear main seal, cam plug or transmission is probably leaking. The leak must be repaired or the new clutch will be ruined.

Installation

If the pilot bearing or bushing was removed, make sure the bore

Installing the pilot bearing into the crankshaft using a suitable driver. *(Courtesy: GM Corp.)*

is free of dirt and burrs that would prevent the bearing/bushing from seating properly. Make sure the bearing/bushing fits properly over the end of the transmission input shaft, then install the new pilot bearing/ bushing using a suitable driver. After installation, apply a thin film of motor oil or high temperature grease to the bushing and transmission input shaft mating surfaces.

If the flywheel was removed, make sure the crank-shaft flange and flywheel mating surfaces are free of rust, dirt and burrs that could cause improper fit and runout. Position the fly wheel on the crankshaft, align- ing the marks made at removal, and install the flywheel bolts. Torque the bolts to specification in a criss-cross pat- tern. Make sure the fly- wheel surface is clean and free of oil or grease.

Lightly grease the clutch disc hub splines and posi- tion the clutch disc on the flywheel. Be careful not to get any grease on the friction lin- ing. Most new clutch discs are marked indicating flywheel side, however if no mark is present, install the clutch disc with the tor- sion spring offset sec- tion facing away from the flywheel. Install a transmission input shaft or clutch alignment tool through the clutch disc and into the pilot bear- ing/bushing.

Make sure the pres- sure plate friction sur- face is clean and free of oil or grease. A new pressure plate may come covered with a preservative to prevent

rust during storage. Remove this preservative using brake clean- ing solvent. Position the pres- sure plate on the clutch disc and flywheel and start the pressure plate bolts. If the same pressure plate is being used, be sure to align the marks made during the removal procedure. Tighten the pressure plate bolts, gradually and evenly, in a criss-cross pat- tern. Once the pressure plate is drawn against the flywheel, torque the bolts to specification. Remove the input shaft or clutch alignment tool.

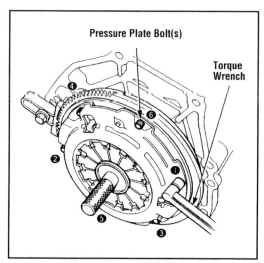

Torque the pressure plate bolts once the pressure plate is snug against the flywheel. *(Courtesy: Honda Motor Co.)*

If removed, lubricate the release lever or clutch fork and pivot and install in the bell hous- ing or transmission. Lightly grease the release bearing to clutch fork contact surfaces and install the release bearing on the fork or lever. Lightly grease the transmission input shaft splines and the surface of the transmis- sion bearing retainer. Install the bell housing and/or transmission. Connect the clutch linkage, adjust the clutch and road test the vehicle.

Bell Housing Alignment

In some rare cases, the bell housing may be damaged, dis- torted, or may have shifted posi- tion when it was reinstalled after a clutch service. Such neglect or damage can misalign the transmission to the engine, and misalignment can cause noise when the clutch is engaged. Misalignment can also cause pulsation in the clutch pedal.

If engine/transmission misalignment is suspected, mount a dial indicator on the flywheel and check the bell housing bore (the rear opening of the bell housing where the transmission fits into the bell housing) for runout. Carefully center the dial indicator in the bore; the tip of the indicator has to touch the inside diameter of the bore. Turn the engine over by hand with a flywheel turning tool and note the runout. If it's out of spec, loosen the bell housing and move it around on its locating dowels in the back of the engine block. Then tighten it up and recheck runout. Offset dowel pins are available for some blocks that allow you to adjust and center the bell housing without too much trial-and-error. Although centering the bell housing sounds like a great deal of extra trouble, it's a necessary step for ensuring smooth clutch performance on some vehicles.

The face of the bell housing (the flat backside where the transmission bolts up) must be flat. If this surface isn't perfectly parallel with the rear of the block, there will be another alignment problem. Reposition the dial indicator so its tip rests on the face of the bell housing and then turn the engine over and watch the indicator. You should be able to correct an out-of-square bell housing by shimming out the 'low' side with shim stock between the bell housing and the block. File any burrs or high spots, and make sure dowel pin locators are in good condition and in place.

Powertrain Mounts

Worn engine and transmission mounts can cause vibration and allow excessive engine and transmission movement. This excessive movement can cause clutch engagement and shifting problems.

Many vehicles have the engine and transaxle assembly, suspension and/or steering components mounted to removable subframes or crossmembers. If the subframe or crossmember is damaged or not properly positioned and secured to the vehicle, this can result in symptoms similar to those caused by worn mounts. Inspect the subframe or vehicle crossmember and the mounting bushings and brackets for wear and damage. If a cross-member or subframe is lowered for engine, transaxle or other system service, it must be correctly reinstalled. Usually there are alignment holes in the body and subframe, which should align if the subframe is installed correctly. Some manufacturers specify that the fasteners be installed and tightened in a certain order. Refer to the vehicle service manual for instructions.

To inspect the mounts on a rear-wheel drive vehicle, carefully raise the engine just high enough to remove the weight from the mounts. This will place a slight tension on the mount's rubber cushion. Repeat the procedure at the transmission to relieve pressure on the rear mount where it attaches to the frame's crossmember.

On a front-wheel drive vehicle, perform the same procedure by raising the powertrain at the various support points along the subframe. If the rubber cushion has separated from the mounting plate, you'll be able to raise the powertrain completely off of the frame. With the weight removed from the mount, look for any signs of cracking, or splitting in the rubber section. Obviously, any of the aforementioned conditions requires that the mount be replaced.

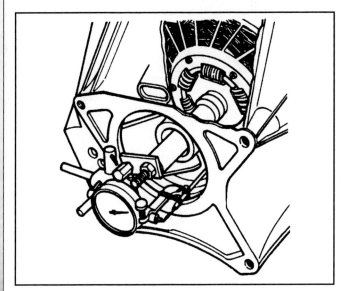

Measuring bell housing bore runout.
(Courtesy: Ford Motor Co.)

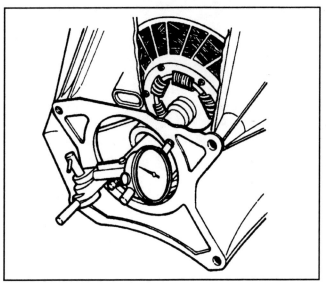

Measuring bell housing face runout.
(Courtesy: Ford Motor Co.)

NOTES

TRANSMISSION DIAGNOSIS AND REPAIR

DESCRIPTION AND OPERATION

The purpose of the transmission is to transfer the engine's power to the driveshaft and the rear wheels. However, one of the shortcomings of an internal combustion engine is that it doesn't develop enough power at low rpm to overcome the inertia of a vehicle. The speed range where it does produce enough power is impractical for maintaining either engine longevity or reasonable fuel economy.

If you were to plot the torque output of an engine throughout its rpm range, you would discover that torque increases as engine speed is increased. However, this only occurs up to a point. After maximum torque is achieved (peak torque), it will begin to fall off even as the engine rpm continues to climb. Since the engine can only develop one torque peak, it's the job of the transmission to manipulate that torque so that maximum power is available through-

out the vehicle's driving range. The transmission accomplishes this torque multiplication by using various combinations of different sized input and output gears. The gear ratio refers to the number of revolutions that the input gear makes in relation to the output gear.

To put the vehicle in motion requires maximum torque multiplication. This is the result when the drive gear is very small and the driven gear is very large. That means that the gear ratio is mathematically high. For example, if the drive gear turns three revolutions for every one revolution of the driven gear, the gear ratio is 3:1. In order to develop torque however, we must sacrifice operating speed. In other words, with a gear ratio of 3:1, output torque is greater than input torque, but output speed is less than input speed. This gear ratio is typical of first gear, when the crankshaft is turning three times as fast as the transmission output shaft. Consequently,

engine rpm remains high while the vehicle speed remains low.

As the input and output gears become closer in size, the operating speeds of each gear become more equal and the effect of torque multiplication is reduced. For example, the gear ratio in second will generally drop to 2:1. As the vehicle gains momentum, the gear ratio is further reduced to a direct drive or 1:1. This is typically a third or fourth gear ratio and means that there is no torque multiplication at all.

Most modern transmissions include an overdrive fifth gear or fifth and sixth gears. Overdrive occurs when the input or drive gear is larger than the output gear. With this gear ratio, torque is actually reduced, but output speed is increased. This setup allows the engine to maintain a lower rpm at increased vehicle speeds. Overdrive gear(s) is typically a 0.75:1 ratio, and not only boosts fuel economy, but reduces engine wear as well.

Reverse is accomplished by

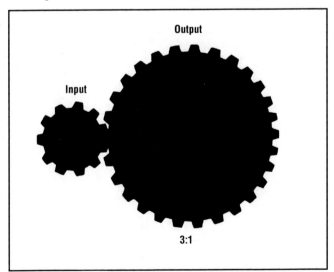

In this illustration, the input (drive) gear is much smaller than the output (driven) gear for an overall ratio of 3:1. This configuration provides torque multiplication since the drive gear must turn three revolutions for every one revolution of the driven gear. However, to gain torque multiplication, output speed is sacrificed.

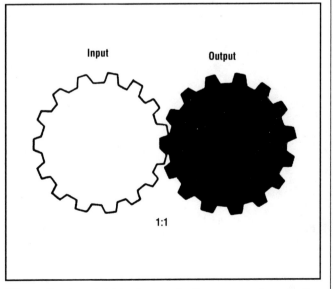

When the input (drive) gear is the same size as the output (driven) gear, no torque multiplication occurs. This is called direct drive and is a 1:1 gear ratio. This arrangement results in input speed and output speed being equal.

Reverse gear can be accomplished by adding another gear, called an idler, to this setup. This causes the output (driven) gear to turn in the opposite direction.

placing an idler gear in between the input and output gears. The idler gear causes the driven gear to rotate in the opposite direction.

Almost all manual transmissions produced today are fully synchronized, constant mesh units. Constant mesh means that all gears are constantly in contact and turning with one another.

Fully synchronized means that there is a system of synchronizer clutches that speed up or slow down the rotation speeds of the shaft and gear, until both are rotating at the same speeds so that both can be locked together without gear clash.

Transmission internal components are housed in an aluminum case. Attached to the case are a side or top cover, extension housing and input shaft bearing retainer. The input shaft projects from the front of the case where the transmission bolts to the bell housing, through the bearing retainer. The input shaft rotates on a ball bearing housed in the front of the case and the bearing retainer.

The countergear, or cluster gear, is located in the bottom of the transmission case and turns on a shaft with roller bearings.

The forward gears and the synchronizer clutches are positioned along the main shaft, or output shaft, which connects to the input shaft and is located above the countershaft. The rear of the main shaft is supported by another roller bearing in the rear of the transmission case.

Reverse gear is located at the rear of the main shaft. A reverse idler gear, located in the transmission case next to the countergear, allows the main shaft to turn in the opposite direction.

The synchronizer clutch assemblies consist of a hub splined to the main shaft, inserts (keys) and insert springs, outer sleeve and blocking rings. There are grooves machined into the sleeves to capture the shift forks, which transfer the motion from the gearshift linkage. Two types of gearshift linkages are used, the internal shift rail/shift fork or external shift rod, either of which is connected to a shift lever mechanism.

DIAGNOSIS

Manual transmissions can suf-

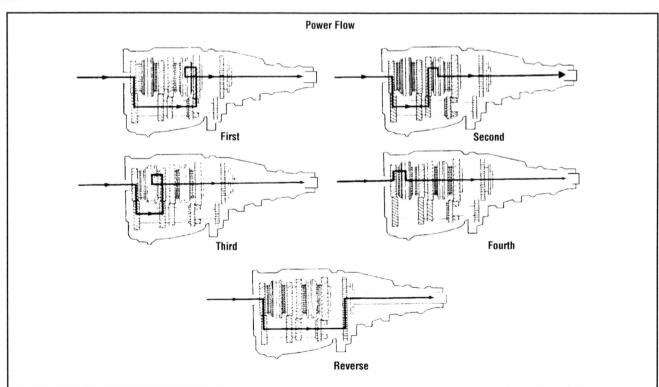

Power flow through a four-speed transmission.

fer from a number of problems; among the symptoms are fluid leaks, noise, hard shifting, gear clash and jumping out of gear. The most common places for fluid leaks are the drain plug, extension housing seal, speedometer drive housing seal, shift lever seal and transmission cover gasket, but the case-to-extension housing gasket, front bearing retainer seal, shift fork seals and cracked or porous castings can also be the source of leaks.

The transmission drain plug can leak if it is loose, stripped or missing a gasket. An extension housing rear seal may leak because the seal has hardened, but it is more likely because the extension housing bushing is worn, allowing the driveshaft slip yoke to wobble. The speedometer drive housing can leak because of a missing or torn O-ring or gasket. Case gaskets can leak because of loose fasteners. Even if fasteners are tight, a blocked vent or overfilling with fluid can cause excessive internal pressure in the transmission, resulting in gasket failure and leaks.

All transmissions make a certain amount of gear noise during normal operation. However, if there is excessive gear whine, check for low fluid level or incorrect fluid. If the fluid type and level are correct and the transmission is still noisy, try to determine the noise based on when it occurs and what it sounds like. If there is only noise when the transmission is in a particular gear, then the problem is with parts associated with that gear. Worn transmission bearings usually make a growling sound, however a bad wheel bearing can also make this sound. The worn transmission bearing will be louder under load, but will quiet or go away when the transmission is in neutral, while the wheel bearing noise would continue.

Before attempting to diagnose shifting problems, try to eliminate causes that are external to the transmission by making sure the clutch is functioning and

adjusted properly, and the shifter linkage is in good shape and adjusted. Adjustment is generally only possible on transmissions with external shift linkage. Inspect the shift linkage as you would mechanical clutch linkage, looking for worn or missing bushings and worn or bent linkage rods; replace parts as necessary.

If the transmission is hard to shift into gear, the problem is usually with the clutch not releasing completely or that the shift linkage is binding or improperly adjusted. Hard shifting can also be caused by a bent shift fork, binding gears and/or synchronizers, or binding between the input shaft and pilot bearing caused by a misaligned bell housing.

Gear clash (grinding noise when shifting from one gear to another) can be caused by a binding pilot bearing, dragging clutch, worn or improperly adjusted shift linkage, or damaged gear teeth or synchronizers. If the transmission jumps out of gear, the cause could be a worn pilot bearing, shift linkage that is worn or out of adjustment, loose or misaligned transmission case or bell housing, worn synchronizers, weak shift rail detent springs, worn shift forks or levers, or worn gear teeth. Even stiff or poor fitting shifter boots have been known to cause a transmission to jump out of gear.

A transmission that is stuck in gear could be the result of shift linkage that is worn, bent or out of adjustment, or broken gears or synchronizer components.

TRANSMISSION SERVICE

In-Vehicle Service

Service to the transmission while it is installed in the vehicle is usually limited to fluid changes, repairing fluid leaks, extension housing bushing replacement, external shift linkage repair and adjustment, and transmission switch and sensor replacement.

Transmission Fluid

To check the fluid level on most vehicles, raise and safely support the vehicle. Clean the area around the transmission fill plug, usually located on the side of the transmission case, and then remove it from the transmission. Most manufacturers specify that the fluid level should be at or slightly below the lower edge of the fill plug hole, but check the service manual to be sure. Stick your finger in the fill plug hole to check the fluid level.

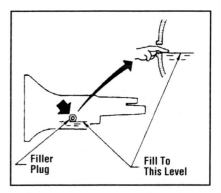

Checking transmission fluid level. *(Courtesy: Nissan Motor Co., Ltd.)*

Also, make sure that the transmission is filled with the proper type of fluid; many manual transmissions require automatic transmission fluid and some use engine oil or hydraulic fluid rather than gear oil. Gear oil specifications can also vary. If in doubt as to the type or quality of the fluid, the transmission fluid should be drained and replaced with the type specified by the vehicle manufacturer. To change the transmission fluid, remove the transmission drain plug and drain the fluid into a clean container. Inspect the fluid for iron and brass particles. Iron particles are most likely from worn gears, while brass particles are from worn synchronizer blocking rings or thrust washers.

After the fluid has completely drained, reinstall the drain plug using a new gasket, if equipped. Fill the transmission to the proper level with the specified lubricant.

Fluid Leaks

Fluid leaks at the extension housing seal, speedometer drive housing and transmission cover can usually be repaired while the transmission is installed in the vehicle. Repairing other leaks may require transmission removal.

If you suspect that there are leaks coming from cracked or porous castings, or if the transmission is so covered in oil that you can't tell where the leak is coming from, clean the transmission thoroughly with a degreasing solvent. After the transmission dries, spray it with an aerosol foot powder. The source of the leak will soon become apparent.

The extension housing seal can be pried from the end of the extension housing, or removed using a suitable puller, after the driveshaft has been removed. Check the driveshaft slip yoke for wear and check its fit in the extension housing bushing. If there is excessive looseness, replace the bushing or the new seal will also leak. Use a suitable puller to remove the old bushing. Install a new bushing and seal using suitable drivers. Lubricate the seal lip before installing the driveshaft slip yoke.

The speedometer drive is usually sealed with an O-ring or gasket. When replacing a transmission cover gasket, inspect the sealing surfaces for nicks or burrs that would prevent proper sealing. Install the cover using a new gasket. If the fastener holes are open to the inside of the transmission case, apply a small amount of sealant to the fastener threads to prevent leaks.

External Shift Linkage

Inspect the shift linkage for cracked or bent rods or levers, worn or missing bushings and elongated bushing holes. Inspect the shifter for wear, binding, looseness and poor lubrication. The shifter is usually replaced as a unit, but linkage rods and levers may be replaced separately. When replacing the shifter, make sure it moves freely in the floor opening and does not bind on the shift boot.

Switches And Sensors

Although a variety of electrical circuits can be connected to manual transmission components, such as that for an upshift light, which tells the driver when to shift for the best fuel economy, the most common electrical components found on a manual transmission are the reverse light switch and the VSS (Vehicle Speed Sensor).

When activated, the reverse light switch completes the circuit for the reverse lights, which help the driver by illuminating the rear of the vehicle when backing up. The reverse light switch can be located either on the transmission, in which case a shift fork closes the switch, or on the shift linkage, where a linkage rod closes the switch. An adjustment may be possible on linkage

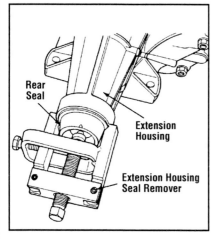

Removing the extension housing seal using a puller.
(Courtesy: Ford Motor Co.)

Rear Seal

Extension Housing

Extension Housing Seal Remover

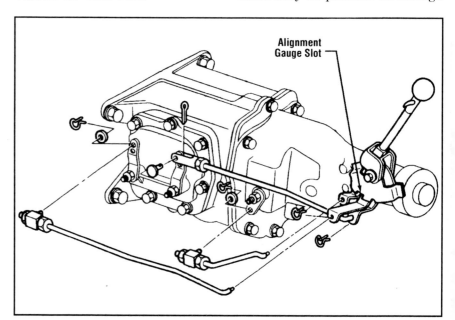

Typical four-speed transmission shifter and shift linkage. Note the position of the alignment gauge slot. *(Courtesy: GM Corp.)*

Alignment Gauge Slot

Linkage adjustment is usually accomplished by inserting an alignment gauge pin into the shifter while it is in neutral, and then adjusting the linkage rods to align with the holes in the shift levers. The linkage clips are then installed. Consult the vehicle service manual for the exact procedure.

mounted switches, so be sure the switch is adjusted properly before condemning it if the reverse lights don't work.

Test the switch function by checking for voltage to the input side of the switch. If voltage is present at the input side, there should be no voltage at the output side of the switch when it is in the open position, but there should be voltage at the output side when the switch is closed. Replace the switch if it does not perform as specified.

Most vehicles with an electronic engine control system have a VSS, which sends an electrical signal to the PCM (Powertrain Control Module) representing the speed of the transmission output shaft. The PCM uses this information, along with that from other sensors, to manage fuel injection and ignition timing. The VSS signal is also used for cruise control and electronic speedometers.

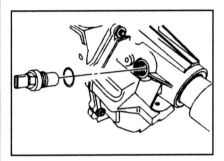

Typical VSS (Vehicle Speed Sensor) installation. *(Courtesy: GM Corp.)*

To test the VSS, raise and safely support the vehicle so the drive wheels are off the ground. Connect the leads of a voltmeter set on the 20-volt AC scale between the sensor output wire and ground. Start the engine and engage the transmission to turn the drive wheels. The indicated voltage on the meter should be 0.5 volts or more, if not replace the sensor. The resistance of the VSS can also be measured with an ohmmeter. Connect the leads across the sensor terminals and compare the reading with the vehicle manufacturer's specifications. Both the VSS and transmission mounted reverse light switch can be replaced by disconnecting the electrical connector and removing the switch/sensor from the transmission. Install the new switch/sensor using a new O-ring coated with transmission fluid. Torque to specification.

Transmission Removal

Disconnect the negative battery cable. It will probably be necessary to tilt the engine back somewhat to remove the transmission, so remove the distributor cap, distributor or any other components that could be damaged by contacting the firewall. Remove the shifter boot from inside the vehicle, as required, for shifter removal.

Raise and safely support the vehicle. Remove the transmission drain plug and drain the fluid into a suitable container.

Mark the position of the rear U-joint on the differential pinion flange, disconnect the U-joint and remove the driveshaft. Remove or lower the exhaust system, and remove splash shields and other components as necessary for transmission removal. If the bell housing is integral with the transmission, remove or disconnect the slave cylinder, disconnect the clutch cable or disconnect the clutch linkage, as required.

If equipped with internal shift linkage, remove the shifter handle. If equipped with external shift linkage, remove the shifter and shift linkage. Disconnect all electrical connectors and the speedometer cable from the transmission.

Support the engine and transmission assembly. Disconnect the transmission mount from the crossmember and remove the crossmember. Lower the engine and transmission assembly enough for access to the transmission mounting bolts and to allow transmission removal.

Make sure the engine is properly supported. Support the transmission and remove the transmission mounting bolts. Slide the transmission straight back until the input shaft clears the clutch disc splines and remove the transmission from the vehicle. Do not allow the weight of the transmission to be supported by the input shaft.

Transmission Disassembly

NOTE: *Procedures for disassem-*

bling and assembling manual transmissions vary according to transmission design. The following is a generalized procedure. Always consult the vehicle service manual for specific procedures and specifications.

Begin transmission disassembly by removing the top or side cover. Rotate the input shaft and examine all the gears as they turn, looking for signs of chipped teeth or other wear. If equipped with external shift linkage, remove the shift forks and shifter shafts from the transmission cover. If equipped with internal shift linkage, remove the shift forks and shift rails.

Remove the extension housing and the input shaft bearing retainer from the transmission case. Remove the reverse idler gear and shaft and remove the main shaft from the transmission case. Remove the input shaft bearing nut and remove the input shaft and front bearing from the case.

Removing the input shaft and front bearing assembly from the transmission case.
(Courtesy: Ford Motor Co.)

Remove the countergear. On some transmissions, the countergear is supported by ball or roller bearings mounted in bearing retainers, which must be removed before the countergear can be removed. On others, the countergear turns on a series of needle roller bearing sets. On this type, drive out the countershaft while supporting the countergear, and then remove the countergear from the transmission case. Keep track of the needle roller bearing sets and any spacers and thrust washers as the countergear is removed from the case.

Remove the necessary retaining clips and snaprings and remove the synchronizer assemblies, gears, bearing and speedometer

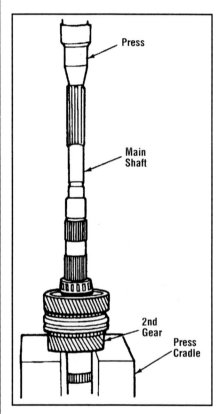

Removing the center bearing from the main shaft.
(Courtesy: Ford Motor Co.)

drive gear from the main shaft. A press will most likely be required to remove the bearings from the main shaft and input shaft. Keep all parts in order as they are removed, so they can be reinstalled correctly.

Before disassembling the synchronizers, scribe marks so the blocking rings can be reinstalled on the same side of the hub and sleeve. Mark the position of the hub in the sleeve before the

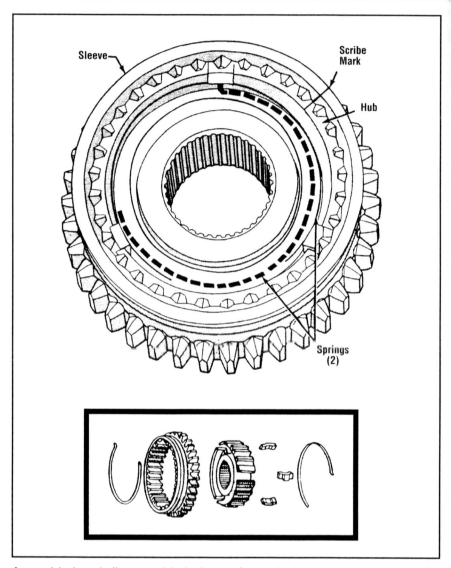

Assembled and disassembled views of a typical synchronizer assembly. Note the scribe mark made so the unit can be reassembled in the same order.

sleeve is removed. Components of synchronizer assemblies should not be interchanged.

Component Inspection

After all internal parts have been removed, check the inside of the transmission case and extension housing for metal chips and shavings. Iron chips are probably from damaged gears. Brass particles could be from damaged synchronizer blocking rings, bushings or thrust washers. Remove and discard all old gasket material, bushings and seals from the case, extension housing and cover(s). Thoroughly clean all

transmission parts in solvent and dry with compressed air.

Inspect the transmission case, extension housing and covers for cracks, worn or damaged bores, stripped threads or other damage, and replace as necessary. Stripped threads can be repaired with suitable thread repair inserts. Inspect the release bearing contact surface of the input shaft bearing retainer for wear. Inspect all machined surfaces for burrs, nicks and gouges that could inhibit sealing or cause misalignment. Small imperfections can be removed with a file or stone.

Contact Pattern	Unacceptable	Acceptable
Desired Pattern (Contact)		
End Contact Pattern		
Traveling Contact (Pattern Moves From Side-To-Side On Face Of Gear)		
High Contact Pattern		
Low Contact Pattern		

Typical transmission gear tooth contact patterns.
(Courtesy: Ford Motor Co.)

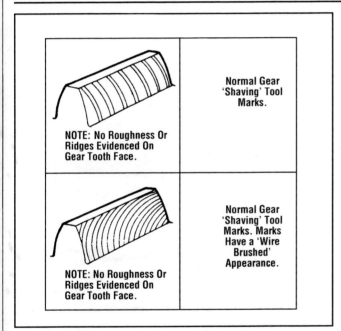

NOTE: No Roughness Or Ridges Evidenced On Gear Tooth Face.	Normal Gear 'Shaving' Tool Marks.
NOTE: No Roughness Or Ridges Evidenced On Gear Tooth Face.	Normal Gear 'Shaving' Tool Marks. Marks Have A 'Wire Brushed' Appearance.

Examples of normal tool marks that may be found on transmission gear teeth. *(Courtesy: Ford Motor Co.)*

Grind Chip/Nick From Corner Face Of Gear-Drive Side. (Approved)	
Grind Chip/Nick From Edge Of Gear OD–May Extend Slightly Into Gear Pattern On Tooth Face. (Approved)	
Grind Chip/Nick From Corner Face Of Gear–Coast Side. (Approved)	
Grind Chip/Nick From Gear Edge May Extend Slightly Into Gear Face. (Approved)	
Grind Chip/Nick From Gear Face–In Gear Pattern Area. (Not Approved)	

Examples of chips or nicks that may be found on transmission gear teeth. *(Courtesy: Ford Motor Co.)*

the transmission input shaft and check for looseness or binding. Replace the input shaft if the splines are worn, damaged or twisted.

Inspect the main shaft splines in the same manner as the input shaft. Make sure the slip yoke can slide freely. Check all main shaft bearing and gear journals for wear or damage and make sure all snapring grooves are square. Mount the main shaft in a lathe fixture or on V-blocks and check runout using a dial indicator. Replace the main shaft if it is damaged or if runout exceeds specification.

Inspect the reverse idler gear

Examine the transmission gear teeth for wear, pits, cracks and chipped teeth. The gear teeth will have a wear pattern and may show factory tool marks. The wear pattern should be in the center of the tooth contact area. Gears with cracked teeth should be replaced, while some chips or nicks can be ground away. The gear blocking ring cone should be smooth and free of nicks or burrs. Synchronizer engagement teeth should be pointed and not rounded off. Check the journal contact surface in the gear bore for damage and check the gear fit on the shaft.

Inspect the input shaft for wear at the tip where it contacts the pilot bearing, check the gear teeth as described in the previous paragraph, and check the splines for rust, burrs or other wear. Slide the clutch disc onto for worn, pitted, cracked, chipped or broken teeth. Check the gear

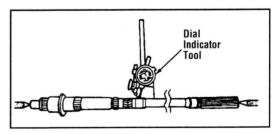

Measuring main shaft runout.
(Courtesy: Ford Motor Co.)

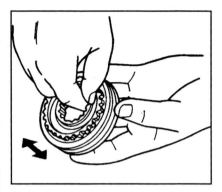

Checking the movement of the synchronizer sleeve over the hub. The sleeve should move easily without force.
(Courtesy: Ford Motor Co.)

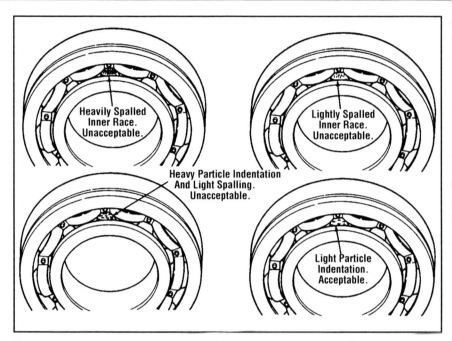

Transmission bearing inspection. *(Courtesy: Ford Motor Co.)*

bore for smoothness and inspect the bearing or bushing the gear rides on as well as the condition of the reverse idler gear shaft.

Examine the synchronizer blocking ring teeth; they should be pointed but smooth and not

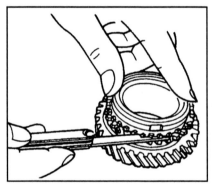

Measuring synchronizer blocking ring-to-gear clearance.
(Courtesy: Ford Motor Co.)

rounded off. The grooves on the inside of the blocking ring where it contacts the gear cone should be clearly defined all the way around and the insert notches should be square. Position the blocking ring squarely on the gear cone and measure the clearance between the ring and gear. Replace the blocking ring if it is worn or the clearance is not within specification. Check the synchronizer hub and sleeve for cracks and spline damage. Make sure the sleeve slides freely on the hub. Check the insert springs

to make sure they are not bent and the hooked ends are not broken off.

Examine the inner and outer transmission bearing races and balls for pits, grooves, discoloration, and spalling or flat spots on the balls, and replace the bearing if any damage is visible. If the bearing looks OK, lubricate it with a bit of light oil. Hold the inner race and rotate the outer race in both directions so the entire surface of both races is covered with light oil. Spin the outer race and feel for roughness as it spins. The race should spin freely and slow down gradually. If the race feels rough or spins freely and then stops spinning suddenly, clean the bearing again and lubricate it. If the bearing still doesn't feel smooth, replace it. Also, hold the bearing sideways (horizontally) and spin the outer race. Even when held horizontally, the bearing should spin freely and smoothly.

Check the shift forks for cracks, bending or excessive wear where they contact the synchronizer sleeves. On vehicles with internal shift mechanisms, inspect the shift rails for damage and bending, which could cause

hard shifting. Check the fit of the shift forks on the rails and the fit of the rails in the transmission case or cover. Also inspect the components of the shift detent mechanism; wear or damage in this area can cause the transmission to jump out of gear.

Examine all remaining transmission components for wear and damage. Parts like loose needle bearings, snaprings, spacers and thrust washers are usually replaced when a transmission is rebuilt and are usually included in an overhaul kit.

Transmission Assembly

NOTE: *Lubricate all shafts, bushings, bearings and thrust washers as they are installed, with the transmission fluid specified by the vehicle manufacturer.*

Begin reassembly by installing the countergear into the transmission case. If the gear rides on sets of needle roller bearings, install the bearings into the countergear bore. The needle roller bearings can be held in place with grease until the countershaft is installed, although using grease along with a

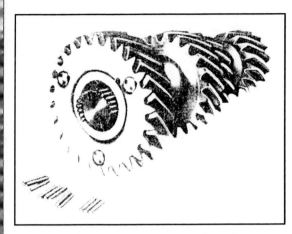

Installing needle roller bearings into the countergear using a dummy shaft.
(Courtesy: GM Corp.)

dummy countershaft is a better solution. The dummy shaft can be made of metal or wood and should be of a slightly smaller diameter than the actual countershaft and shorter in length to allow the countergear to be placed in position in the case. Position the countergear in the

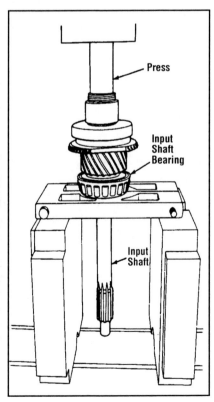

Installing the input shaft bearing onto the input shaft.
(Courtesy: Ford Motor Co.)

transmission case along with the appropriate thrust washers and install the countershaft. As the countershaft is tapped into place, the dummy countershaft will be driven out.

Once the countergear is installed, check the end-play using a dial indicator. If the end-play is not within specification, spacers or thrust washers of a different thickness must be installed to adjust the end-play.

Press the input shaft bearing onto the input shaft and install the input shaft in the transmission case. Assemble the synchronizer assemblies, aligning the scribe marks made during the removal procedure. Install the gears, synchronizer assemblies and main shaft bearing on the main shaft. Press the bearing into position and install the necessary snaprings. Install the speedometer drive gear on the main shaft.

Position the reverse idler gear in the transmission case with the thrust washer. Install the roller bearings into the input shaft and hold in place with grease, if necessary. Carefully install the main shaft into the case, making sure it properly contacts the input shaft roller bearing. Check the main shaft end-play using a dial indicator and adjust play as necessary. Clearance where the main shaft engages the input shaft is critical as this can affect the shift into fourth gear. Excessive clearance can also cause the transmission to jump out of fourth gear.

Install a new seal, if equipped, in the input shaft bearing retainer and install the retainer to the case with a new gasket. Install a new bushing and seal in the extension housing and install the housing to the transmission case using a new gasket. Install the speedometer drive gear housing using a new gasket or O-ring,

as required.

Install the shift mechanism and shift forks to the transmission or transmission cover, using new O-rings where required. Install the cover to the transmission using a new gasket. If equipped with external shift linkage, make sure the shift forks properly engage the synchronizer sleeves. Install the transmission drain plug.

Transmission Installation

Lightly lubricate the end of the input shaft and the input shaft splines with grease. Also lightly grease the input shaft bearing retainer and release bearing contact surfaces. If the bell housing is integral with the transmission, lubricate the release bearing lever, or clutch fork, pivot and install the lever/fork. Install the release bearing in the lever/fork.

Raise the transmission into position, align the input shaft and clutch disc splines, then slide the transmission forward until the input shaft engages the pilot bearing and the transmission case is seated on the bell housing or the bell housing is seated on the rear of the engine block. Do not force the transmission into place and never let it hang by the input shaft. If the transmission will not install properly, remove it and determine the problem. Check clutch disc alignment using an old input shaft or clutch alignment tool.

Once the transmission is in place, install and tighten the mounting bolts. Raise the engine and transmission and install the transmission mount and crossmember. If equipped with external shift linkage, install the shifter assembly and adjust the linkage. If equipped with internal shift linkage, install the shift handle.

Connect all electrical connectors and the speedometer cable. If the bell housing is integral with the transmission, install or connect the slave cylinder, connect the clutch cable or connect the clutch linkage, as required.

Install the exhaust system and any splash shields or other components that were removed for transmission access.

Lightly grease the driveshaft slip yoke exterior and splines and slide it onto the transmission output shaft. Align the rear U-joint and the differential pinion flange with the marks made at removal, and secure the U-joint using the bolts, caps or U-bolts, as required.

Fill the transmission to the proper level with the required fluid, install the transmission filler plug, and then lower the vehicle. Install the shifter boot and any engine compartment components that were removed or repositioned. Connect the negative battery cable and road test the vehicle.

NOTES

TRANSAXLE DIAGNOSIS AND REPAIR

DESCRIPTION AND OPERATION

A manual transaxle performs the same function as a manual transmission; it transfers the engine's power to the wheels. However, where a transmission works in conjunction with a separate driveshaft and differential to accomplish this, the transaxle incorporates the transmission and differential in one housing. Manual transaxles are most commonly used on front-wheel drive cars, but they have also been used in the rear of some performance cars and older economy cars.

The transmission part of the transaxle functions similarly to the transmission in a rear-wheel drive vehicle, except in the transaxle, the input and main, or output, shafts are positioned along side one another, and there is no countergear. The input and main shaft are mounted in either ball bearings or tapered roller bearings. The gears on the main shaft are meshed with those on the input shaft, and are engaged by the synchronizer assemblies, the hubs of which are splined to the main shaft. When the transaxle is shifted, the shift fork moves the synchronizer sleeve, which drives the inserts, or keys, and the blocking ring onto the gear cone. The action of the blocking ring pressing on the gear cone brings the gear to the same turning speed, allowing the splines on the synchronizer sleeve to engage and lock into the synchronizer gear teeth, locking the gear to the main shaft.

Most transaxles are mated to engines that are positioned transversely in the vehicle, where the centerline of the crankshaft is parallel to the drive axles, or halfshafts. In this design, a helical pinion gear is located at the end of the main, or output, shaft and drives a helical ring gear, which is mounted to

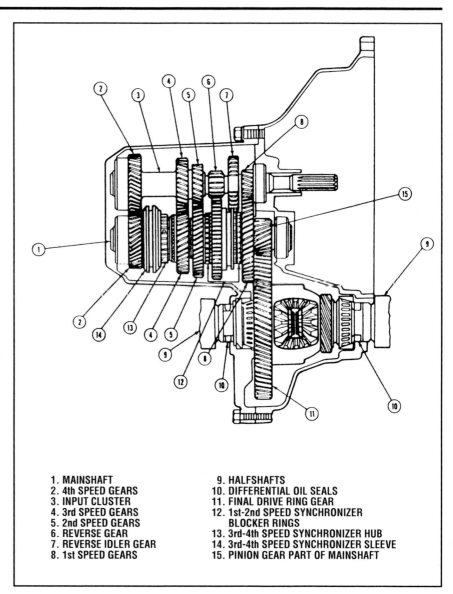

1. MAINSHAFT
2. 4th SPEED GEARS
3. INPUT CLUSTER
4. 3rd SPEED GEARS
5. 2nd SPEED GEARS
6. REVERSE GEAR
7. REVERSE IDLER GEAR
8. 1st SPEED GEARS
9. HALFSHAFTS
10. DIFFERENTIAL OIL SEALS
11. FINAL DRIVE RING GEAR
12. 1st-2nd SPEED SYNCHRONIZER BLOCKER RINGS
13. 3rd-4th SPEED SYNCHRONIZER HUB
14. 3rd-4th SPEED SYNCHRONIZER SLEEVE
15. PINION GEAR PART OF MAINSHAFT

Cross-sectional view of a typical manual transaxle used in a transverse engine front-wheel drive vehicle.

the differential.

Transaxles that are used with engines that are mounted longitudinally, where the crankshaft is perpendicular to the halfshafts, drive a hypoid pinion and ring gear in the differential, which changes the output direction to the wheels. A drive chain and sprockets are sometimes used with this design to transfer power from the crankshaft to the

transaxle input shaft. The differential is also sometimes housed in a separate case, with a separate fluid supply, that bolts onto the transaxle case.

Power is transferred from the differential to the vehicle's wheels with the drive axles, or halfshafts. A stub axle is splined into the differential side gear and is connected to an intermediate shaft by a CV-joint. Another CV-joint is attached to the other end of the intermediate shaft, which is in turn connected to another stub shaft that is splined into the wheel hub. CV-joints will be discussed in the next section of this study guide.

Most manual transaxles are shifted using external shift linkage. A shifter assembly is mounted on the floor of the vehicle and rods or cables transfer the shifter motion to the shift levers mounted on the transaxle.

DIAGNOSIS

Manual transaxle problems include fluid leaks, noise, vibration, hard shifting, gear clash and jumping out of gear. The most common places for fluid leaks are the transaxle case section and cover (if equipped) mating points, switch, sensor or cable adaptors, and the differential seals, however, the input shaft bearing seal and shift lever seals can also be the source of leaks.

The transaxle drain plug can leak if it is loose, stripped or missing a gasket. Speed sensor, reverse light switch and speedometer cable adaptors can leak because of a loose fitting, or missing or torn O-ring or gasket. Case gaskets can leak because of loose fasteners. Even if fasteners are tight, a blocked vent or overfilling with fluid can cause excessive internal pressure in the transaxle, resulting in gasket failure and leaks. Seals can leak due to wear, age or excessive clearance in associated bearings or bushings.

All transaxles make a certain amount of gear noise during normal operation. However, if there is excessive gear whine, check for low fluid level or incorrect fluid. If the fluid type and level are correct and the transaxle is still noisy, try to determine the noise based on when it occurs and what it sounds like. If there is only noise when the transaxle is in a particular gear, then the problem is with parts (gear, synchronizer assembly) associated

with that gear. If there is noise in all gears, suspect worn or damaged input or output gears or bearings. Worn transaxle bearings usually make a growling sound, however a bad wheel bearing can also make this sound. The worn transaxle bearing will be louder under load, but will quiet or go away when the transmission is in neutral, while the wheel bearing noise would continue.

If noise is more prevalent in a turn, the cause may be worn differential side gears, however a clicking noise in a turn would be caused by a worn outboard CV-joint. Clunking noise during acceleration or deceleration could be caused by loose engine/transaxle mounts, a worn inboard CV-joint, or a worn differential pinion shaft.

Excessive vibration can be caused by bad wheel bearings, out-of-round or unbalanced tires, a damaged halfshaft or worn CV-joint, or incorrect halfshaft operating angle. Vibration can also be caused by worn engine/transaxle mounts.

Before attempting to diagnose shifting problems, try to eliminate causes that are external to the transaxle by making sure the clutch is functioning and adjusted properly, and the shifter and shift linkage is in good shape and adjusted. A shifter that is worn or linkage that is worn, binding or not adjusted properly can cause excessive shift effort, inability to shift into gear or may allow the transaxle to jump out of gear. Worn or incorrectly positioned engine/transaxle mounts can also cause binding or other problems with the shift linkage.

If the transaxle is hard to shift into gear, the problem is usually with the clutch not releasing completely or that the shift linkage is binding or improperly adjusted. Hard shifting can also be caused by damaged transaxle internal shift mechanism components (shift lever, shift fork, shift rail, etc.).

TRANSAXLE SERVICE

In-Vehicle Service

Although there are transaxle designs that allow some service of internal components with the transaxle in the vehicle, in most cases the transaxle must be removed from the vehicle for repair. Service that can be performed with the transaxle in the vehicle is usually limited to fluid changes, leak repairs, shifter and shift linkage repair and adjustment, transaxle mount replacement and transaxle switch and sensor replacement.

Transaxle Fluid

Transaxle fluid level should be checked with the engine off and the vehicle parked on a level surface. Refer to the vehicle service manual to see whether the fluid level should be checked with the fluid cold or at normal operating temperature.

If the transaxle is equipped with a dipstick, clean the area around the dipstick and remove it from the transaxle case. Wipe off the gauge and reinstall the dipstick in the transaxle. Remove the dipstick and check the fluid level on the gage. Add fluid, as required, to bring the fluid level to the full level.

If the fluid level is checked at the filler plug, clean the area around the filler plug and remove it from the transaxle case. Most manufacturers specify that the fluid level should be at or slightly below the lower edge of the filler plug hole, but check the service manual to be sure. Stick your finger in the filler plug hole to check the fluid level. If the fluid level is low, add fluid until it starts to run out the filler plug hole, then reinstall the filler plug and torque to specification.

Make sure that the transaxle is filled with the proper type of fluid; many manual transaxles require automatic transmission fluid and some use engine oil or hydraulic fluid rather than gear oil. Gear oil specifications can also vary. If in doubt as to the

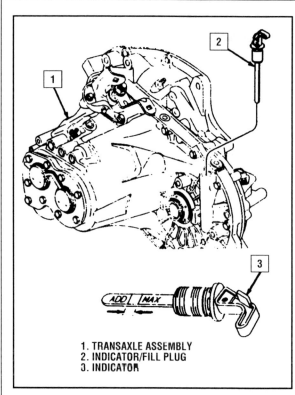

1. TRANSAXLE ASSEMBLY
2. INDICATOR/FILL PLUG
3. INDICATOR

Checking transaxle fluid level with a dipstick. *(Courtesy: GM Corp.)*

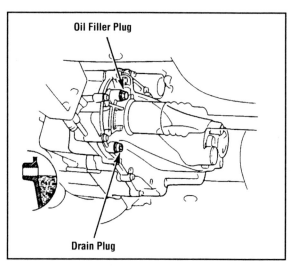

Typical transaxle filler and drain plug locations. *(Courtesy: Honda Motor Co.)*

type or quality of the fluid, the transaxle fluid should be drained and replaced with the type specified by the vehicle manufacturer.

To change the transaxle fluid, raise and safely support the vehicle, then remove the transaxle drain plug and drain the fluid into a clean container. Inspect the fluid for iron and brass particles. Iron particles are most likely from worn gears, while brass particles are from worn synchronizer blocking rings or thrust washers.

After the fluid has completely drained, reinstall the drain plug using a new gasket, if equipped. Fill the transaxle to the proper level with the specified lubricant.

Fluid Leaks

Fluid leaks from speed sensor, reverse light switch and speedometer cable adaptors can usually be repaired by replacing torn or damaged gaskets or O-rings, or applying Teflon tape to the threads of fittings and tightening them. If fluid is leaking from a cover that can be removed with the transaxle in the vehicle, inspect the sealing surfaces of the case and cover for nicks or burrs that would prevent proper sealing. Install the cover using a new gasket or sealant, as required. If the fastener holes are open to the inside of the transaxle case, apply a small amount of sealant to the fastener threads to prevent leaks.

If a differential seal is leaking, the inner CV-joint or halfshaft stub shaft must first be removed from the differential. For halfshaft removal and installation, refer to the Driveshaft/ Halfshaft and Universal Joint/ Constant Velocity Joint Diagnosis and Repair section of this study guide.

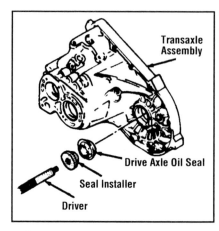

Differential seal installation. *(Courtesy: GM Corp.)*

The inner CV-joint can be attached to the transaxle differential in a variety of ways. Most often there is a circlip in a groove on the end of the inner CV-joint stub shaft, which retains the inner CV-joint to the differential side gear. However, on some vehicles the inner CV-joint is bolted to a stub shaft and flange that extends from the transaxle differential, while on others the inner CV-joint is retained by a snapring, which must be removed from inside the differential. Because of these variations, always consult the vehicle service manual for the exact replacement procedure.

Once the halfshaft and/or stub shaft is removed, pry the old seal from the differential using a suitable tool. Install the new seal using a seal installer. Lubricate the seal lip before installing the halfshaft or stub shaft.

Shift Linkage

The external transaxle shift linkage can be either a system of linkage rods or cables attached to a floor mounted shifter. Inspect the shifter assembly for loose mountings, looseness or binding in the mechanism and lack of lubrication. Tighten loose mountings and lubricate as required. Replacement parts for worn components may be available or the shifter assembly may be replaced as a unit.

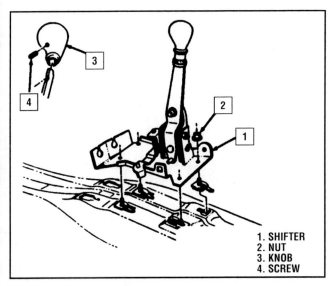

1. SHIFTER
2. NUT
3. KNOB
4. SCREW

Typical cable type floor shifter assembly.
(Courtesy: GM Corp.)

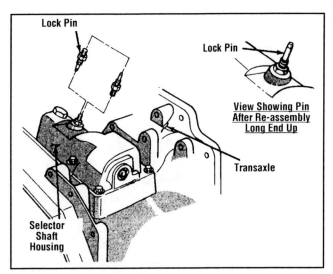

Lock pin used for pinning a manual transaxle in the neutral position for shift linkage adjustment.
(Courtesy: DaimlerChrysler Corp.)

Inspect linkage rods for cracks, bending, worn or missing bushings, loose, worn or missing linkage rod mounting bolts or pins, and lack of lubrication. Replace worn or damaged components and lubricate pivot points, as required. Adjustment procedures will vary according to manufacturer, but generally a pin or drill bit is used to hold the transaxle in neutral while the linkage is adjusted.

Examine shift cables for fraying and damage to the cable ends, binding, kinked or misrouted cable housings, or other damage. Replace worn or damaged cables. It may be necessary to remove the shift boot, console and carpeting for access to the cables. To adjust the cables, the transaxle and shifter assembly are usually pinned in the neutral position with the cable adjusters loosened, then the cable adjusters are tightened.

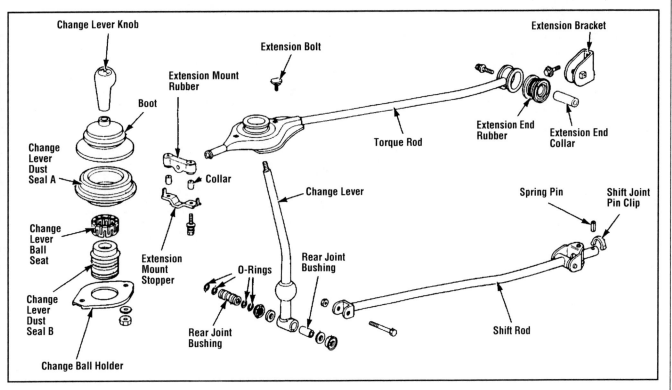

Exploded view of a typical shifter and linkage rod assembly.   (Courtesy: Honda Motor Co.)

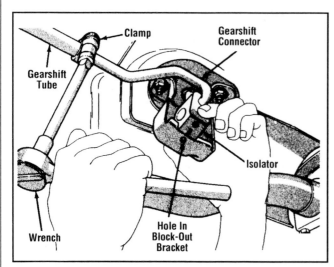

Shift linkage rod (gearshift tube) adjustment. On this transaxle, the rib on the isolator is aligned with the hole in the block-out bracket with the transaxle pinned in neutral, then the clamp bolt is tightened. *(Courtesy: DaimlerChrysler Corp.)*

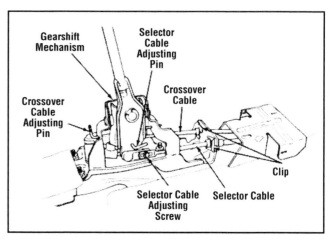

Pinning the shifter assembly for shift cable adjustment. *(Courtesy: DaimlerChrysler Corp.)*

Transaxle Mounts

Worn engine and transaxle mounts can cause vibration and allow excessive engine and transaxle assembly movement. This excessive movement can adversely affect clutch and shift linkages, possibly resulting in clutch slippage, hard shifting, inability to shift into gear or jumping out of gear.

Many vehicles have the engine and transaxle assembly, suspension and/or steering components mounted to removable subframes or crossmembers. If the subframe or crossmember is damaged or not properly positioned and secured to the vehi-

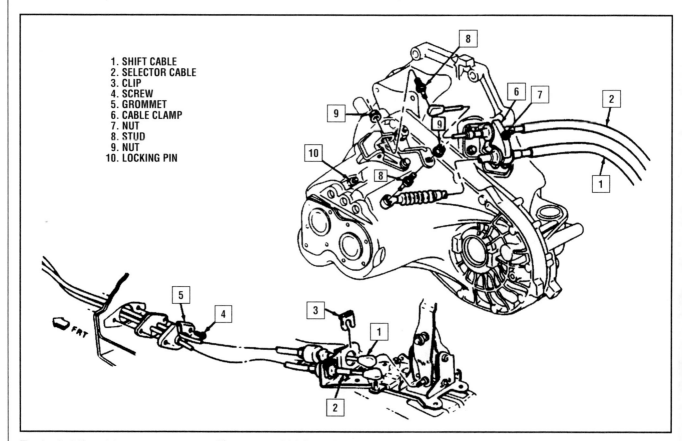

1. SHIFT CABLE
2. SELECTOR CABLE
3. CLIP
4. SCREW
5. GROMMET
6. CABLE CLAMP
7. NUT
8. STUD
9. NUT
10. LOCKING PIN

Typical shift cable arrangement. *(Courtesy: GM Corp.)*

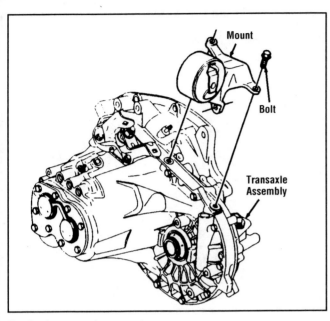

Typical transaxle mount.
(Courtesy: GM Corp.)

cle, this can result in symptoms similar to those caused by worn mounts. Inspect the subframe or vehicle crossmember and the mounting bushings and brackets for wear and damage. If a crossmember or subframe is lowered for engine, transaxle or other system service, it must be correctly reinstalled. Usually there are alignment holes in the body and subframe, which should align if the subframe is installed correctly. Some manufacturers specify that the fasteners be installed and tightened in a certain order. Refer to the vehicle service manual for instructions.

To check the transaxle mounts, pull up and push down on the transaxle while watching the mount. If the rubber separates from the metal plate of the mount or if the transaxle moves up but not down, meaning the mount is bottomed out, the mount must be replaced. Also make sure that the mount is not loose on the mounting bracket or frame due to loose fasteners.

To replace a transaxle mount, first disconnect the negative battery cable, and then properly support the engine/transaxle assembly with a hoist or jack.

Raise the engine/transaxle assembly enough to take the weight off the mount. Remove the mount fasteners and remove the mount from the transaxle and frame or bracket.

Position the new mount and tighten the mount fasteners. Refer to the vehicle service manual for proper mount and subframe or crossmember alignment instructions, as well as tightening sequences and specifications. Remove the hoist or jack and connect the negative battery cable.

Switches And Sensors

Although a variety of electrical circuits can be connected to manual transaxle components, such as that for an upshift light, which tells the driver when to shift for the best fuel economy, the most common electrical components found on a manual transaxle are the reverse light switch and the VSS (Vehicle Speed Sensor).

When activated, the reverse light switch completes the circuit for the reverse lights, which help the driver by illuminating the rear of the vehicle when backing up. The reverse light switch is usually located on the transaxle case, and a shift fork acts on the switch to close it.

Test the switch function by checking for voltage to the input side of the switch. If voltage is present at the input side, there should be no voltage at the output side of the switch when it is in the open position, but there should be voltage at the output side when the switch is closed.

Replace the switch if it does not perform as specified.

Most vehicles with an electronic engine control system have a VSS, which sends an electrical signal to the PCM (Powertrain Control Module) representing the speed of the transmission output shaft. The PCM uses this information, along with that from other sensors, to manage fuel injection and ignition timing. The VSS signal is also used for cruise control and electronic speedometers.

To test the VSS, raise and safely support the vehicle so the drive wheels are off the ground. Connect the leads of a voltmeter set on the 20-volt AC scale between the sensor output wire and ground. Start the engine and engage the transaxle to turn the drive wheels. The indicated voltage on the meter should be 0.5 volts or more, if not replace the sensor.

The resistance of the VSS can also be measured with an ohmmeter. Connect the leads across the sensor terminals and compare the reading with the vehicle manufacturer's specifications.

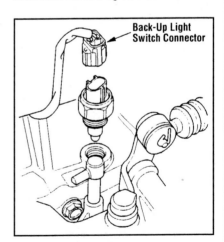

Typical reverse light switch installation.
(Courtesy: Honda Motor Co., Ltd.)

Both the VSS and reverse light switch can be replaced by disconnecting the electrical connector and removing the switch/sensor from the transaxle. Install the new switch/sensor using a new O-ring coated with transmission fluid. Torque to specification.

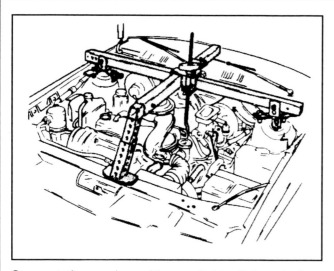

Support the engine with a suitable fixture before transaxle removal.
(Courtesy: GM Corp.)

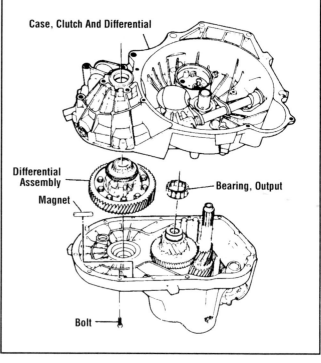

Removing the bell housing/differential housing case from the transaxle case.
(Courtesy: GM Corp.)

Transaxle Removal

NOTE: The following procedure is an example of transaxle removal with the engine left supported in the vehicle. However, some manufacturers specify that the engine and transaxle be removed from the vehicle as a unit and then separated. Always consult the vehicle service manual for the proper procedure.

Disconnect the negative battery cable. Remove the air cleaner assembly and air intake tube. Disconnect the speedometer cable and label and disconnect the electrical connectors from the transaxle. Disconnect the clutch cable or remove the slave cylinder from the bell housing.

Install a suitable engine support fixture. Raise and safely support the vehicle, then remove the front wheels. Remove the necessary splash shields and disconnect the exhaust pipe from the exhaust manifold. Remove the drain plug and drain the transaxle fluid into a container. Remove the halfshafts.

NOTE: Some vehicles may require that locator plugs be installed when the halfshafts are removed from the differential side gears. If these plugs are not installed, the gears can become misaligned.

Remove the starter and the lower bell housing cover, if equipped. Disconnect the shift control rods or shift cables from the transaxle, as required. Support the transaxle with a suitable jack.

Disconnect and remove the necessary engine and transaxle-to-frame mounts, brackets and cross-member or subframe. Remove the trans-axle-to-engine mounting bolts and slide the transaxle away from the engine until the input shaft clears the clutch pressure plate. Lower the transaxle from the vehicle.

Transaxle Disassembly

NOTE: Procedures for disassembling and assembling manual transaxles vary according to transaxle design. The following is a generalized procedure. Always consult the vehicle service manual for specific procedures and specifications.

Clean the outside of the transaxle case and position it in a suitable holding fixture to facilitate disassembly. Remove all sensors and switches from the transaxle case.

Remove the clutch release bearing. Remove the external shift levers, shift control covers and detent mechanisms. Remove the mounting bolts and separate the bell housing/differential housing from the main transaxle case. Keep track of any input and main shaft end-play shims. Remove the differential assembly from the transaxle case. Mark the position of each differential side bearing preload shim and race for assembly reference.

Remove the shifter shaft assembly from the transaxle case. Remove the end cover from the transaxle case, keeping track of any input shaft and main shaft shims. Remove the main shaft and input shaft and gear assemblies along with the shift rail assemblies from the transaxle case.

Remove the necessary snaprings and remove the bearings, gears and synchronizer assemblies from the input shaft and main shaft. A press will most likely be required. Keep all parts in order as they are removed, so they can be reinstalled correctly.

Before disassembling the synchronizers, scribe marks so the blocking rings can be reinstalled on the same side of the hub and sleeve. Mark the position of the hub in the sleeve before the sleeve is removed. Components of synchronizer assemblies should not be interchanged.

Component Inspection

After all internal parts have been removed, check the inside of the bell housing/differential housing case and transaxle case for metal chips and shavings. Iron chips are probably from damaged gears, while brass particles could be from damaged synchronizer blocking rings. Remove and discard all old gasket material, sealant and seals from the cases. Thoroughly clean all transaxle parts in solvent and dry with compressed air.

Inspect the transaxle case, bell housing/differential housing case and covers for cracks, worn or damaged bearing race bores, worn bushings, stripped threads or other damage, and replace as necessary. Stripped threads can be repaired with suitable thread repair inserts. Inspect all machined surfaces for burrs, nicks and gouges that could inhibit sealing or cause misalignment. Small imperfections can be removed with a file or stone.

Inspect the transaxle bearings for pits, grooves, discoloration, and roughness of rotation. Inspect the bearing races for scoring, wear or evidence of overheating. Replace parts as necessary. Bearings and races must always be replaced as an assembly, and if an original bearing is reused, it must be mated with the same original race.

Examine the transaxle gear teeth for wear, pits, cracks and broken teeth. The gear blocking ring cone should be smooth and free of nicks or burrs. Synchronizer

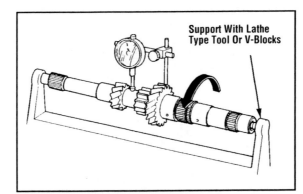

Measuring transaxle shaft runout. *(Courtesy: Honda Motor Co.)*

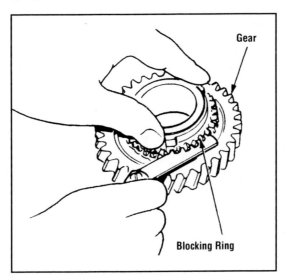

Measuring synchronizer blocking ring-to-gear cone clearance. *(Courtesy: Honda Motor Co.)*

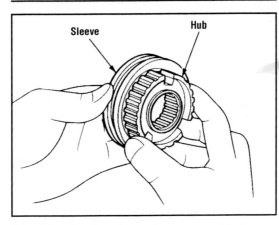

Checking for freedom of movement between the synchronizer hub and sleeve. *(Courtesy: Honda Motor Co.)*

engagement teeth should be pointed and not rounded off. Check

the journal contact surface in the gear bore for damage and check the gear fit on the shaft.

Inspect the input shaft for wear at the tip where it contacts the pilot bearing, and check the splines for rust, burrs or other wear. Slide the clutch disc onto the input shaft and check for looseness or binding. Check the input shaft and main shaft gears for wear, pits, cracks and broken teeth. Check all input and main shaft bearing and gear journals for wear or damage, measure their diameters and compare to specification, and make sure all snapring grooves are square. Mount the shafts in a lathe fixture or on V-blocks and check runout using a dial indicator. Replace the input or main shaft if it is worn, damaged or if runout exceeds specification. Replace the input shaft if the splines are worn, damaged or twisted.

Examine the synchronizer blocking ring teeth; they should be pointed but smooth and not rounded off. The grooves on the inside of the blocking ring where it contacts the gear cone should be clearly defined all the way around and the insert notches should be square. Position the blocking ring squarely on the gear cone and measure the clearance between the ring and gear. Replace the blocking ring if it is worn or the clearance is not within specification. Check the synchronizer hub and sleeve for cracks and spline damage. Make sure the sleeve slides freely on the hub. Check the insert springs to make sure they are not bent and the hooked ends are not broken off.

Check the shift forks for cracks, distortion or excessive wear where they contact the synchronizer sleeves. Inspect the shift rails for scoring and distortion. Check the fit of the rails in the transaxle case bushings or bearings. Also inspect the components of the shift detent mechanism; wear or damage in this area can cause the transaxle to jump out of gear.

Remove the lock pin bolt and remove the cross differential pin from the differential, then remove the side gears, pinion gears and thrust washers. Inspect the differential ring gear, side gear and pinion gear teeth for scuffed, nicked, burred or broken teeth. Inspect the thrust washers for wear, nicks and scuffs. Inspect the differential side bearings for pits, grooves, discoloration, and roughness of rotation. Inspect the differential for cracks, distortion or other damage. Replace any worn or damaged parts.

Transaxle Assembly

NOTE: *Lubricate all shafts, bushings, bearings and thrust*

1. BEARING, DIFFERENTIAL
2. CARRIER, ASSEMBLY DIFFERENTIAL
3. CARRIER, DIFFERENTIAL
4. PIN, CROSS DIFFERENTIAL
5. WASHER, THRUST PINION GEAR
6. WASHER, THRUST SIDE GEAR
7. GEAR SIDE DIFFERENTIAL
8. GEAR, PINION DIFFERENTIAL
9. SCREW, 9NM (84 LB IN.)
10. WASHER, LOCK
11. GEAR, RING DIFFERENTIAL
12. GEAR, SPEEDO (MECHANICAL)
13. GEAR, SPEEDO (ELECTRONIC)
14. BEARING, DIFFERENTIAL
15. BOLT

Exploded view of a typical transaxle differential.
(Courtesy: GM Corp.)

washers as they are installed, with the transmission fluid specified by the vehicle manufacturer.

Use suitable drivers to install the necessary bushings, bearings, races and seals in the transaxle cases. Assemble the synchronizer assemblies, aligning the scribe marks made during the removal procedure. Install the gears, synchronizer assemblies and bearings on the input and main shafts and install the necessary snaprings. Assemble the shift rail and fork assemblies.

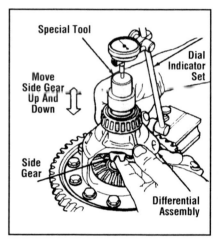

Measuring differential side gear end-play.
(Courtesy: DaimlerChrysler Corp.)

Press new bearings onto the differential carrier, as required. If removed, install the ring gear to the carrier and torque the bolts to specification. New bolts should be used. Install the pinion and side gears in the differential carrier with the thrust washers. Check side gear end-play using a dial indicator and correct using different thickness thrust washers if end-play is not within specification. After end-play adjustment, install the cross differential pin and the lock pin bolt. Torque the bolt to specification.

Input and main shaft end-play as well as differential bearing preload must be adjusted to specification. These adjustments are made using selective fit shims. The procedure for determining

Dimension A — Selected Shim Can Be 0.03 mm (0.001 in.) Above Or 0.12 mm (0.004 in.) Below The End Plate Mounting Surface

PART NO.	DIM. A mm (IN.)
14092067	4.54 (0.179)
14092068	4.64 (0.183)
14092069	4.74 (0.187)
14092070	4.84 (0.191)
14092071	4.94 (0.194)
14092072	5.04 (0.198)
14092073	5.14 (0.202)

End Plate Mounting Surface

Dim. A

1

2

1. Bearing, Output Shaft Support
2. Retainer, Bearing 70 Nm (50 lb ft.)

Using a depth micrometer to determine main shaft bearing shim thickness.
(Courtesy: GM Corp.)

shim size varies according to transaxle design and manufacturer. Shaft end-play may be determined using a dial indicator or by measuring with a depth micrometer. Bearing preload may be determined by measurement using special tools or by measuring turning torque with a torque wrench.

Install the shifter shaft assembly into the transaxle case. Install the input and main shaft assemblies with the shift rail assembly in the transaxle case with the input and output shaft bearings and any required shims. Install the shim, bearing race and differential assembly in the case. Install a new gasket or apply a bead of sealant on the case flange, as specified by the manufacturer. Install any required input and main shaft shims along with the differential bearing shim and bearing race in the bell housing/differential housing case and install the case to the transaxle case. Install the mounting bolts and torque to specification.

Install the transaxle end cover and any bearing shims. Install the external shift levers, shift control covers and detent mechanisms. Install the sensors and switches to the transaxle case, using new gaskets or O-rings, as required.

Transaxle Installation

Lightly lubricate the end of the input shaft and the input shaft splines with grease. Also lightly grease the input shaft bearing retainer and release bearing contact surfaces. Lubricate the release bearing lever and the inside bore of the release bearing and install the release bearing in the lever.

Raise the transaxle into position, align the input shaft and clutch disc splines, then slide the transaxle toward the engine until the input shaft engages the pilot bearing and the transaxle bell housing is seated on the engine block. Do not force the transaxle into place. If the transaxle will not install properly, remove it and determine the problem. Check clutch disc alignment using an old input shaft or clutch alignment tool.

Once the transaxle is in place, install and tighten the mounting bolts. Connect and install the necessary engine and transaxle-to-frame mounts, brackets and crossmember or subframe. Refer to the vehicle service manual for proper mount and subframe or crossmember alignment instructions, as well as tightening sequences and specifications. Remove the transaxle support jack.

Connect the shift control rods or shift cables to the transaxle, as required. Install the starter and the lower bell housing cover, if equipped. Lubricate the differential seal lips. Install the half-shafts, making sure the clips on the stubs shafts fully engage in the differential side gears.

Connect the exhaust pipe to the exhaust manifold and install

Inch-Pound Torque Wrench

Special Tool

C-Clamp

Measuring differential bearing turning torque.
(Courtesy: DaimlerChrysler Corp.)

the splash shields. Install the front wheels and lower the vehicle. Remove the engine support fixture. Connect the clutch cable or install the clutch slave cylinder. Adjust the cable or bleed the clutch hydraulic system, as required. Adjust the transaxle shift linkage.

Connect the transaxle electrical connectors and the speedometer cable. Install the air cleaner assembly and air intake tube. Connect the negative battery cable. Fill the transaxle with the proper type and quantity of fluid. Road test the vehicle.

NOTES

DRIVESHAFT/HALFSHAFT AND UNIVERSAL JOINT/CONSTANT VELOCITY (CV) JOINT DIAGNOSIS AND REPAIR (FRONT- AND REAR-WHEEL DRIVE)

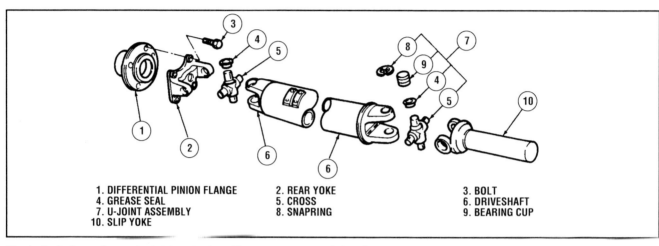

1. DIFFERENTIAL PINION FLANGE	2. REAR YOKE	3. BOLT
4. GREASE SEAL	5. CROSS	6. DRIVESHAFT
7. U-JOINT ASSEMBLY	8. SNAPRING	9. BEARING CUP
10. SLIP YOKE		

Exploded view of a typical driveshaft. *(Courtesy: Ford Motor Co.)*

DESCRIPTION AND OPERATION

Driveshaft And Universal Joints

The driveshaft transfers power from the transmission to the differential on a rear-wheel drive vehicle. The driveshaft consists of a hollow metal tube with universal joints at each end, each of which is attached to yokes at the transmission and differential.

The universal joints, or U-joints, allow the driveshaft to move up and down in response to movement in the rear suspension. The cross and roller joint, or cardan U-joint is the most common type of universal joint used. The cardan U-joint consists of a center cross, four bearing cups, each containing a set of needle roller bearings, grease seals and snaprings. Two of the bearing cups, opposite one another, are pressed into a yoke, which is welded onto each end of the driveshaft tube. The snaprings fit into grooves in the yokes to retain the bearing cups, however on some vehicles the cups are retained at the factory by injected plastic. The cross rotates on the roller bearings.

The other bearing cups on the front U-joint are attached to a slip yoke, which moves in and out on the splines of the transmission main, or output, shaft. This in-and-out movement is necessary because as the suspension moves, the distance between the transmission and differential changes. The bearing cups on the front U-joint can either be pressed into the slip yoke and retained with snaprings, or can be attached with bolts and metal straps or U-bolts. The rear U-joint bearing cups can either be pressed into a yoke, which in turn, is bolted to the differential pinion flange, or can be attached to the flange yoke with bolts and metal straps or U-bolts.

When a cardan U-joint is driven at an angle, its output

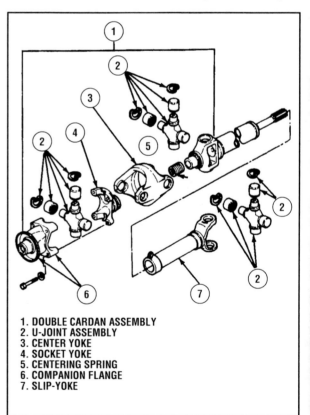

1. DOUBLE CARDAN ASSEMBLY	
2. U-JOINT ASSEMBLY	
3. CENTER YOKE	
4. SOCKET YOKE	
5. CENTERING SPRING	
6. COMPANION FLANGE	
7. SLIP-YOKE	

Exploded view of a double cardan U-joint assembly. *(Courtesy: Ford Motor Co.)*

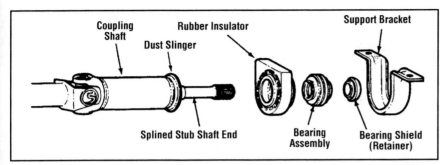

Exploded view of a typical center support bearing assembly. *(Courtesy: Ford Motor Co.)*

speed increases and decreases during each revolution. If driven at a sharp angle, this speed fluctuation can result in torsional vibration. In applications where the operating angle is too great for a single U-joint to handle, or in order to reduce torsional vibration, a constant velocity (CV) joint, or double cardan U-joint is used. This type of CV-joint should not be confused with the type of CV-joint used with halfshafts on front-wheel drive applications, which will be discussed later in this section. The double cardan joint consists of two cross and roller joints connected by a centering socket and center yoke. The two U-joints counteract the output shaft speed fluctuations, with the second U-joint canceling the shaft speed changes of the first U-joint.

If the distance between the transmission and differential is too great for one driveshaft, two driveshafts joined at a center support bearing are used. The center support bearing bracket is mounted to the vehicle frame and houses a bearing and rubber insulator.

Halfshaft And Constant Velocity Joints

Halfshafts transfer power from the transaxle to the front wheels on a front-wheel drive vehicle. They are also used on some vehicles with rear-wheel drive and independent rear suspension to transfer power from the differential to the rear wheels. The halfshaft consists of a stub shaft (which can also be part of the inboard CV-joint) that is splined into the differential side gear, another stub shaft that is splined into the wheel hub, an interconnecting shaft, and two CV-joints, which connect the interconnecting shaft to the stub shafts.

The CV-joints allow the halfshafts to move up-and-down in response to suspension movement and, in the case of front-wheel drive vehicles, allow for steering movement in the wheels. Because of this and the fact that halfshafts are more compact than regular drive-shafts, these CV-joints must be able to operate at angles far more extreme than that which could be handled by a cardan or even a double cardan U-joint. The term constant velocity can be applied to these joints because they turn continually at the same speed at all operating angles, unlike cardan joints, which, as indicated earlier, speed up and slow down during rotation.

There are two types of CV-joints, the ball-type joint and the tripod-type joint. The ball-type joint consists of a star shaped inner race, which is splined to the interconnecting shaft, six balls, a cage, an outer race, which is usually part of the stub shaft, and a boot. The tripod-type joint consists of a spider, which is splined to the interconnecting shaft, three rollers that turn on needle roller bearings located between the spider and rollers, a housing, or yoke, that is part of the stub shaft, and a boot.

Both CV-joint types can be either fixed joints or plunging joints. In a plunging joint, the tri-

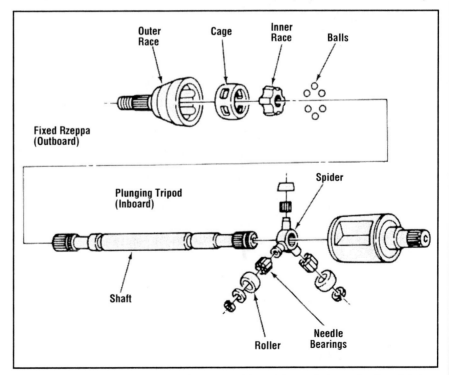

Exploded view of a halfshaft assembly with an inboard tripod joint. *(Courtesy: Ford Motor Co.)*

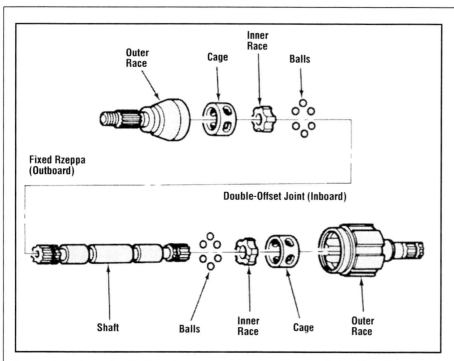

Exploded view of a halfshaft assembly with an inboard double offset joint. *(Courtesy: Ford Motor Co.)*

pod rollers or ball bearings move in and out on elongated grooves in the yoke or outer race. This movement is necessary because as the suspension moves up-and-down, the distance between the transaxle (differential on rear-wheel drive applications with independent suspension) and the wheel changes. The tripod rollers or ball bearings do not move in-and-out on a fixed joint.

The inboard CV-joint is a plunging joint and the outboard joint is a fixed joint on front-wheel drive applications. On rear-wheel drive vehicles with independent suspension, one CV-joint can be fixed and the other plunging, or both can be plunging joints.

Fixed ball-type joints are also known as Rzeppa joints. Plunging ball-type joints can be either double offset or cross groove joints.

Front-Wheel Drive Wheel Bearings

Two types of wheel bearings are commonly used on front-wheel drive vehicles. The more common type is a ball or roller bearing that is pressed into the steering knuckle with the wheel hub pressed into the bearing. This type of bearing can be sealed or may require packing with wheel bearing grease during assembly. If bearing replacement is required, usually the steering knuckle must be removed from the vehicle.

The other type of bearing, which is becoming more common on newer vehicles, is a sealed ball or roller bearing that is integral with the wheel hub. The hub/bearing assembly bolts onto the steering knuckle, making replacement much simpler.

An example of an integral hub and bearing assembly. *(Courtesy: GM Corp.)*

DIAGNOSIS AND INSPECTION

Driveshaft And Universal Joints

The most common symptoms of driveshaft and U-joint problems are noise and vibration. Perform a thorough road test and listen for noise under all driving conditions. A worn U-joint will make a squeaking or grinding noise, most likely because it has become dry. Without lubricating grease, the dry needle roller bearings wear grooves in the bearing surfaces of the cup and cross.

A knocking or clunking sound can be caused by an extremely worn U-joint, differential problems, or excessive clearance between the driveshaft slip yoke and the output shaft or extension housing bushing. A worn center support bearing can make a growling or whining sound.

Driveshaft vibration can be caused by binding U-joints, an unbalanced condition, or incorrect driveshaft angle. Vibration during heavy acceleration or deceleration, especially at lower speeds, is probably due to incorrect driveshaft angle. When there is a vibration that is difficult to isolate, road test the vehicle and note the rpm at which the vibration is most noticeable. Suppose the vibration is worst at 1500 rpm in high gear. Change the speed of the driveshaft itself by running the engine to 1500 rpm in first gear and second gear. If the

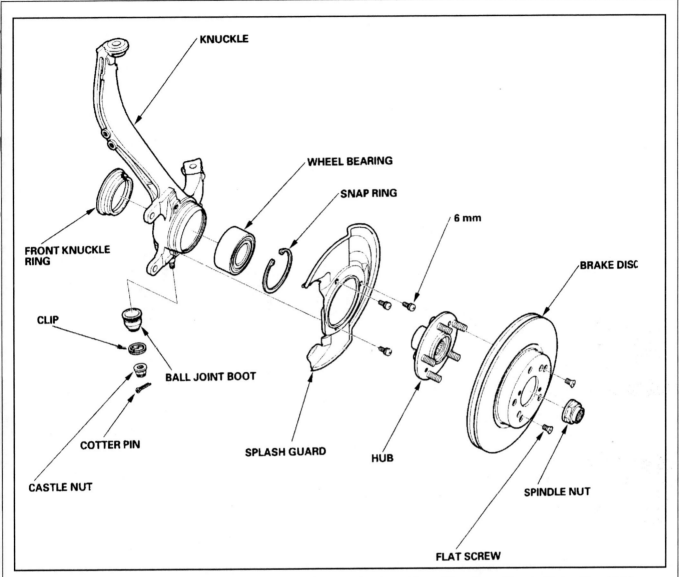

KNUCKLE

WHEEL BEARING

SNAP RING

6 mm

FRONT KNUCKLE RING

BRAKE DISC

CLIP

BALL JOINT BOOT

COTTER PIN

SPLASH GUARD

HUB

CASTLE NUT

SPINDLE NUT

FLAT SCREW

An example of a wheel bearing that is pressed into the steering knuckle. *(Courtesy: Honda Motor Co., Ltd.)*

---

vibration still feels the worst at 1500 rpm, the cause is not in the driveshaft. If the intensity of the vibration changes when the engine is doing 1500 rpm in each gear, then the driveshaft may be at fault.

Raise and safely support the vehicle. Inspect the driveshaft for dents or other obvious physical damage. Look for any clean spots on the driveshaft that could indicate a missing balance weight, and look for accumulations of mud or undercoating, all of which could upset driveshaft balance.

Check for worn U-joints by turning the driveshaft and slip yoke or pinion yoke in opposite directions, and by moving the driveshaft up-and-down in the yoke. If there is any movement in the U-joint, it must be replaced. Sometimes, particularly in the case a of a binding U-joint, the only way to judge U-joint condition is to remove the driveshaft from the vehicle and check the U-joints through their range of motion. Be sure to scribe alignment marks between the rear U-joint or yoke and the differential pinion shaft yoke, prior to removal, so the driveshaft can be reinstalled in the same position.

While the driveshaft is installed, move the slip yoke up-and-down in the transmission extension housing. If there is movement, remove the driveshaft and examine the surface of the slip yoke for wear. If the yoke appears OK, then the extension housing bushing is worn. Also examine the condition of the slip yoke and transmission output shaft splines and check the fit of the yoke on the output shaft.

On vehicles with two-piece driveshafts, noise and vibration can be caused by a dislocated or faulty center bearing support insulator, worn center support bearing or excessive compression of the rubber insulator. Vibration and noise can also be

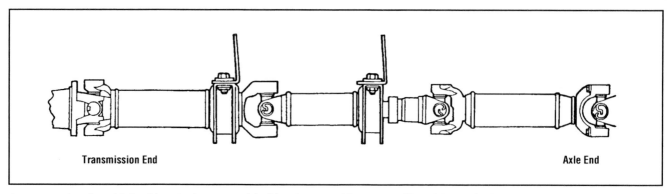

An example of multiple driveshafts assembled in phase. *(Courtesy: Ford Motor Co.)*

caused by a seized driveshaft slip yoke spline, causing the rubber insulator to be pulled out of the center bearing support. On vehicles with multiple driveshafts and center support bearings, the driveshafts must be installed with the U-joint yokes on the same plane, 'in phase', or the assembly will be imbalanced resulting in vibration.

Inspect the center support bearing by rotating the inner race while holding the outer race. Replace the bearing if there is evidence of wear or roughness. Inspect the center support rubber insulator for hardening, cracking and deterioration, and replace if necessary.

Measuring Driveshaft Runout

If the driveshaft and U-joints pass initial inspection and there is a vibration problem, check the driveshaft for a bent condition using a dial indicator. Sand around an area at the front, center and rear of the driveshaft so the indicator foot rides on a smooth surface. Position the indicator perpendicular to the driveshaft and zero it. Turn the driveshaft and compare the measurement to specification.

If runout is beyond specification at the front or center measuring locations on a one-piece driveshaft, the driveshaft must be replaced. However, if the front and center measurements are within specifications but the rear is not, mark the rear runout high point using a crayon. Remove the driveshaft from the differential pinion flange and position it 180 degrees from its original position. On some vehicles, the differential pinion flange is circular, in which case the driveshaft can be reposi-

tioned in 45 degree increments. Recheck the driveshaft runout. If runout is now within tolerance, road test and check for vibration. If vibration is still present, reposition the driveshaft slip yoke 180 degrees on the transmission output shaft and road test. If there is still vibration, then the driveshaft must be balanced.

If when driveshaft runout was rechecked, the runout was still beyond specification, again mark the high point with a crayon. Excessive driveshaft runout can be caused by the driveshaft itself or by the differential pinion flange. If the two high point marks are within about an inch of one another, the driveshaft is bent and must be replaced. However, if the marks are about 180 degrees apart, then the yoke or pinion flange is responsible.

Mark the position of the U-

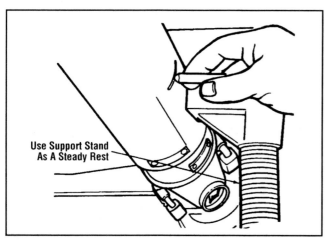

Marking the rear driveshaft runout high point. *(Courtesy: Ford Motor Co.)*

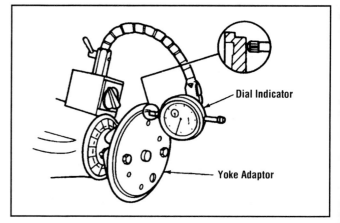

Measuring pinion yoke runout using a dial indicator and adaptor tool. *(Courtesy: Ford Motor Co.)*

joint or yoke on the differential pinion flange or yoke, and then remove the driveshaft. Check pinion flange or yoke runout using a dial indicator. To check runout on a yoke, a round adaptor will need to be installed, Check runout at the front and at the edge of the flange or adaptor.

If runout exceeds specification, remove the pinion flange or yoke and reposition 180 degrees from its original position. Pinion bearing preload must be checked before the pinion flange or yoke is removed, so that the pinion nut can be reinstalled properly. Recheck the pinion flange or yoke runout. If it is still excessive, replace the flange or yoke. If runout is excessive with the replacement flange or yoke, it will be necessary to replace the ring and pinion gear set.

Driveshaft Balancing

If driveshaft runout is within specification and there is still vibration, driveshaft imbalance can be corrected while the driveshaft is in the vehicle by installing screw-type hose clamps on the driveshaft.

Raise and safely support the vehicle. Support the drive axle so the driveshaft is in its normal operating position. Remove the rear wheels and retain the drums or rotors with the lug nuts. Run the engine, in gear, until the speedometer reads 40-50 mph. Carefully bring a piece of chalk or crayon up to the

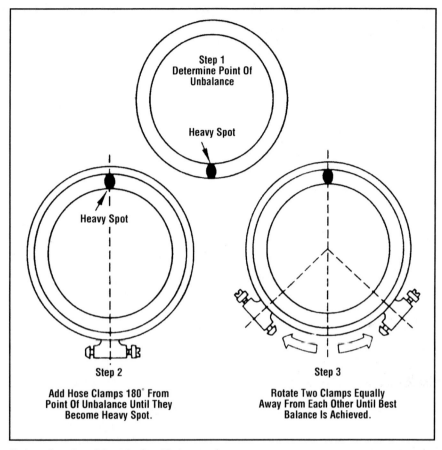

Balancing the driveshaft with hose clamps.

driveshaft at the rear of the shaft, until it just makes contact; this mark will indicate the heavy side of the driveshaft. Install and tighten two hose clamps on the driveshaft with their heads positioned 180 degrees from the heavy spot mark.

Again run the engine, in gear at the same speed, and check for

vibration. If vibration is still present, rotate the clamps approximately 45 degrees away from one another and recheck. If necessary, continue to rotate the clamps apart in smaller increments until vibration is eliminated or reduced.

If the vibration is still not eliminated, repeat the procedure at

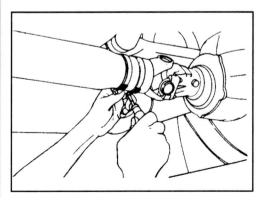

Adjusting the positions of the hose clamps on the driveshaft.
(Courtesy: Ford Motor Co.)

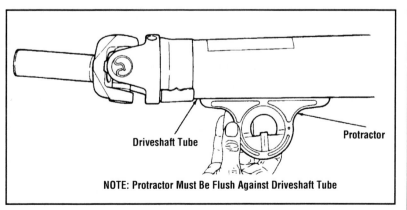

Measuring driveshaft angle using a spirit level protractor.
(Courtesy: Ford Motor Co.)

the front end of the driveshaft. Install the wheels, lower the vehicle and road test.

Checking Driveline Angle

Incorrect driveline angles can also cause vibration. The most common cause of driveline angle problems is incorrect vehicle ride height, however if the vehicle ride height is at specification and driveline angle is incorrect, shims can be used under the transmission mount or at the rear axle spring seats.

Before checking the driveline angle, jounce the vehicle to settle the suspension in the normal load position, then check the vehicle ride height. Refer to the vehicle service manual for measuring points and specifications. If the ride height is not within specification, correct as necessary before proceeding further.

Driveline angle can be measured using special gauges or with a spirit level protractor. Place the gauge or protractor on the bottom of the vehicle frame and zero the gauge or protractor. Check the engine/transmission angle by positioning the gauge or protractor on a U-joint bearing cup or yoke ear of the driveshaft slip yoke, and compare the reading to specification. If the reading is not within specification, check the engine mounts for

damage and repair as necessary. It may be necessary to loosen the engine mounts, raise the engine and lower it back into position, and then retorque all fasteners. Recheck the engine/transmission angle, and if it is still not within specification, install shims between the transmission mount and crossmember until the angle is correct.

Check the driveshaft angle and pinion angle by positioning the gauge or protractor on the U-joint bearing cups or yoke ears of the driveshaft and differential pinion flange. If either or both readings are not within specification, correct by placing shims between the rear springs and the rear axle spring seats or between the rear axle and control arms.

Halfshaft And Constant Velocity Joints

Noise and vibration are the most common symptoms of faulty Constant Velocity (CV) joints, and torn CV-joint boots are the most common reason for CV-joint failure. Outboard CV-joints usually wear more quickly than inboard joints because the outboard joint operates at much more extreme angles than inboard joints.

Inspect the CV-joint boots for tears and punctures. An accumulation of grease on components in

the vicinity of the CV-joint boot is a sure sign that the boot is torn and centrifugal force has pushed grease out of the opening in the boot. A torn boot is usually cause for joint replacement or at the very least disassembly and inspection. Just as grease can escape through the tear, dirt and grit can enter. The loss of lubricant coupled with the introduction of abrasives into the moving joint will quickly cause the joint to fail.

If the CV-joint boots pass inspection, road test the vehicle. If a clicking or snapping noise is heard when accelerating around a corner, suspect a worn outboard CV-joint. A clunk during acceleration or deceleration could be caused by a worn inboard CV-joint. Vibration or shudder during acceleration can also be caused by a worn inboard joint.

Front-Wheel Drive Wheel Bearings

Wheel bearings can wear due to excessive use or from lack of lubrication. When wheel bearings wear, the balls or rollers and races become grooved, pitted, scored or otherwise damaged. These deformities can cause a humming or growling noise as the wheel turns during vehicle operation.

To check for worn or loose wheel bearings, raise and safely support the vehicle. Rotate the wheel by hand and listen and feel for roughness. Grasp the tire at the top and bottom and check for excessive play in the bearing. If in doubt, remove the wheel and secure the brake rotor to the wheel hub using the lug nuts. Mount a dial indicator on the steering knuckle, with the stylus resting on the wheel hub. Move the brake rotor in and out to check bearing end-play. Replace the bearing if play is not within specification.

SERVICE

Driveshaft Removal And Installation

Raise and safely support the

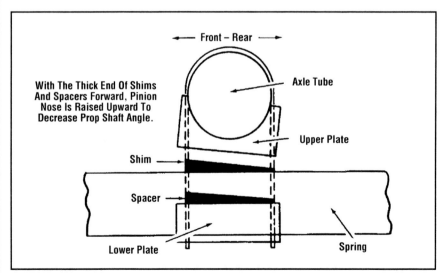

Using shims to correct driveshaft and/or pinion angle.
(*Courtesy: Ford Motor Co.*)

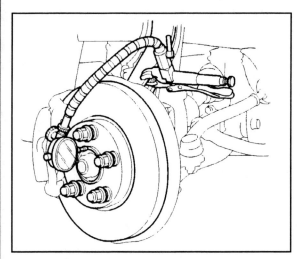

(Checking wheel bearing end-play with a dial indicator. *(Courtesy: Honda Motor Co., Ltd.)*

vehicle. Mark the position of the rear U joint or yoke on the differential pinion yoke, for assembly reference. Remove the bolts, strap bolts or U-bolts, as required, and remove the driveshaft from the differential pinion yoke.

On two piece driveshafts, support the rear driveshaft section while loosening and removing the center support bearing mounting bolts. Do not allow the rear driveshaft section to hang from the center support bearing. Pull the slip yoke from the transmission extension housing and remove the driveshaft from the vehicle.

Inspect the U-joints, slip yoke and center support bearing, if equipped, for wear and damage. Replace parts as necessary.

Lubricate the slip yoke splines and extension housing bushing and seal contact areas with grease, then slide the slip yoke into the transmission extension housing. On two-piece driveshafts, support the driveshaft and install the center support bearing mounting bolts.

Install the rear U-joint or yoke to the differential pinion yoke, aligning the marks made during removal. Install the yoke mounting bolts, U-joint strap bolts or U-bolts, as equipped. Tighten all fasteners to specification.

U-Joint Replacement

Place the driveshaft in a vise, being careful not to damage it. Mark the position of the slip yoke and rear U-joint yoke, if equipped, in relation to the driveshaft tube yokes, so they can be reinstalled in the same position.

Remove the snaprings that retain the bearing cups in the yokes at each end of the driveshaft, and then reposition the driveshaft in the vise so the yoke is between the jaws. Place a socket slightly smaller than the bearing cup on one side between the bearing cup and vise jaw, and place a socket larger than the bearing cup on the other side.

Slowly tighten the jaws of the vise so that the smaller socket forces the cross and the opposite bearing cup out of the driveshaft and into the larger socket. Remove the driveshaft from the vise and remove the socket from over the bearing cup. The bearing cup should be forced out of the yoke enough to grip and remove with pliers.

Drive the cross in the opposite direction in the same manner, in order to make the opposite bearing cup accessible, and pull it free with pliers. Use this procedure to remove all bearing cups from the yokes. Remove the crosses once the bearing cups are removed. On double cardan joints, remove the socket yoke, centering yoke and spring.

Thoroughly clean all dirt and foreign material from the bearing cup bores and snapring grooves in the yokes. Use a stone or file to remove any burrs that could hinder installation of the new joint.

Remove the bearing cups from opposite ends of the new U-joint and start one of the cups into the driveshaft yoke. Install the cross inside the yoke and slide one end into the bearing cup. Position the yoke in the vise, then slowly close the vise jaws until the bearing cup is pressed into the yoke. Loosen the jaws and position the smaller socket between one of the jaws and the bearing cup, then tighten the jaws so the cup is pressed in far enough to install the snapring in the groove.

Open the vise and start the other bearing cup in the other side of the yoke. Press the bearing cup in the same manner as the first one, making sure the cross is in line with the bearing cup as it is pressed in.

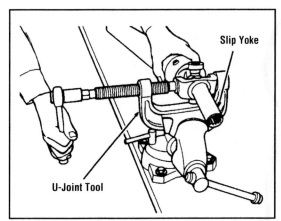

Slip Yoke

U-Joint Tool

Removing a bearing cup from the driveshaft slip yoke. Here a special U-joint tool is shown, however, the same results can be obtained with a vise and sockets.
(Courtesy: Ford Motor Co.)

CAUTION: It is very easy to damage or misalign the needle roller bearings in the bearing cup if the cross is not kept in line with the bearing cup during assembly. If the U-joint binds easily or the bearing cup cannot be pressed in far enough to install the snapring, then one or more roller bearings has probably fallen to the bottom of the bearing cup. Remove the bearing cup, reposition the roller bearings and reinstall.

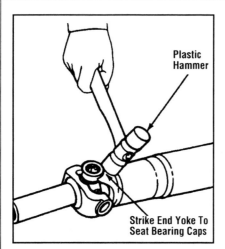

If there is some binding in the U-joint, strike the yoke with a brass or plastic hammer to seat the bearing cups. Support the shaft end when doing this and do not strike the bearing cups.
(Courtesy: Ford Motor Co.)

Install all remaining U-joint cups in the same manner. When installing the slip yoke and rear yoke, align the marks that were made during removal. On double cardan joints, pack the socket relief and ball with chassis grease and install a new seal on the centering ball stud. Make sure all snaprings are properly installed.

Check the U-joints for freedom of movement. If there is some slight binding, a sharp rap on the yoke with a brass or plastic hammer will seat the bearing cups. Take care to support the shaft end and do not strike the bearing cups. Make sure the U-joints are free to rotate easily without binding before installing the driveshaft. If supplied, install the grease fittings and grease the U-joints.

Halfshaft Removal

With the wheels on the ground, loosen the hub retainer nut. Raise and safely support the vehicle. Remove the wheel and remove and discard the hub retainer nut.

Disconnect the tie-rod end from the steering knuckle and remove the disc brake caliper. Support the caliper out of the way with wire; do not let the caliper hang from the brake hose. Disconnect the lower ball joint from steering knuckle.

Pull outward on the steering knuckle while pulling the halfshaft stub shaft from the hub. If the stub shaft will not pull free, do not hammer on the stub shaft, but use a suitable puller to remove the shaft from the hub. Do

not allow the halfshaft to hang unsupported. If necessary, wire it up to keep it from hanging.

If the inboard stub shaft is part of the inboard CV-joint and is retained in the differential side gear with a circlip, use a suitable prybar or slide hammer/puller tool to release the joint from the differential side gear, then remove the halfshaft from the vehicle. Never pull on the axle shaft in an effort to separate the stub shaft from the differential; the inboard joint can be pulled apart.

If removing both halfshafts, some vehicles require that locator plugs be installed in the sides of the differential to keep the side gears from becoming dislocated. If the gears were to become misaligned, the differential might have to be removed from the transaxle to realign the gears.

If the inboard CV-joint is bolted to the inboard stub shaft, mark the position of the mounting flanges in relation to each other. Remove the fasteners and remove the halfshaft from the vehicle.

Do not lower the vehicle and attempt to move it with the halfshafts removed, as the wheel

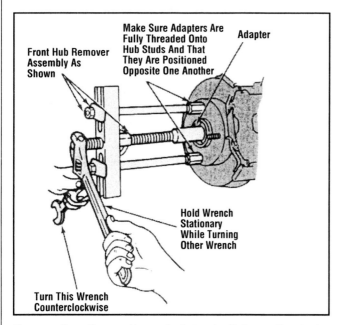

Separating the outboard stub shaft from the hub.
(Courtesy: Ford Motor Co.)

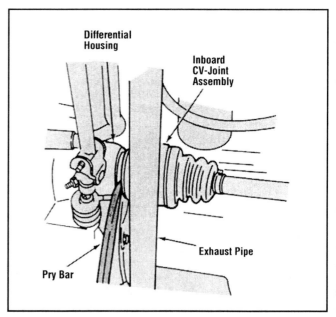

Using a prybar to remove the inboard CV-joint from the differential. *(Courtesy: Ford Motor Co.)*

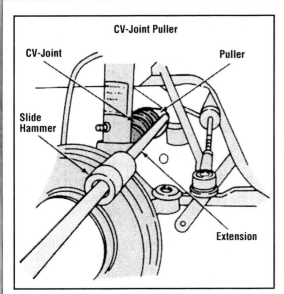

CV-Joint Puller

Using a slide hammer/puller tool to remove the inboard CV-joint from the differential. *(Courtesy: Ford Motor Co.)*

bearings could become damaged. If it is necessary to move the vehicle with the halfshafts removed, install dummy stub shafts and torque the axle nuts.

Halfshaft Installation

If the inboard stub shaft is part of the inboard CV-joint, install a new circlip on the stub shaft. Lightly lubricate the splines and the differential seal contact area with grease. Remove the locator plugs if they were installed during the removal procedure. Align the stub shaft and differential side gear splines, then push the halfshaft into the differential until the circlip seats in the groove in the differential side gear.

If the inboard CV-joint is bolted to the inboard stub shaft, align the marks on the mounting flanges, install the fasteners and torque to specification.

Pull outward on the steering knuckle and install the outboard CV-joint stub shaft into the hub. If the stub shaft will not seat in the hub, use a suitable puller tool to draw it into place; do not use the hub retainer nut.

Connect the lower ball joint to the steering knuckle and connect the tie-rod end. Install the brake caliper. Install the wheel and install a new hub retainer nut.

Lower the vehicle. Torque the hub retainer nut to specification. On some vehicles the nut must be staked in place with a dull chisel. Check the transaxle fluid level and fill as necessary.

CV-Joint Replacement

Ball-Type CV-Joint

NOTE: The following describes a generalized procedure. Always consult the vehicle service manual for specific instructions.

Secure the interconnecting shaft in a vise with soft jaw covers. Mark the location of the small end of the boot on the shaft for assembly reference. Use side cutter to cut the large boot clamp and remove the clamp from the boot. Roll the boot back over the shaft.

Angle the CV-joint to expose the inner race. Free the joint from the shaft by hitting the inner race with a brass drift and hammer. Support the joint as it comes off the shaft to keep it from falling. Remove and discard the boot.

Mark the relationship between the outer race, cage and inner race using paint or a marker, for assembly reference. Press down on one side of the inner race to tilt the cage, then remove the balls from the cage. If the balls are tight in the cage, use an old screwdriver with blunt edges to pry the balls from the cage. Be careful not to scratch or damage the balls or cage.

Pivot the cage and inner race

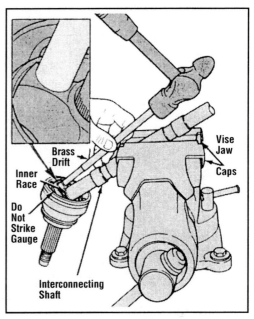

Removing a ball-type CV-joint from the interconnecting shaft. *(Courtesy: Ford Motor Co.)*

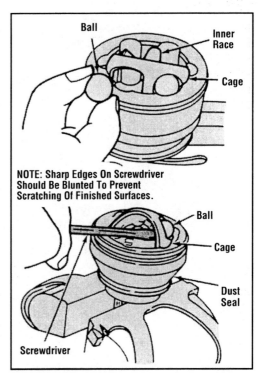

NOTE: Sharp Edges On Screwdriver Should Be Blunted To Prevent Scratching Of Finished Surfaces.

Removing the balls from the cage on a ball-type CV-joint. *(Courtesy: Ford Motor Co.)*

until they are perpendicular to the centerline of the outer race. Make sure the cage windows are aligned with the lands of the outer

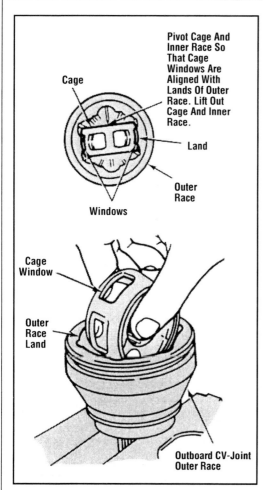

Removing the cage and inner race from the outer race on a ball-type CV-joint. *(Courtesy: Ford Motor Co.)*

after the inner race and cage are installed in the outer race.

Install a new boot on the shaft. Position the end of the boot in the groove or in the position marked prior to disassembly. Install a new clamp and tighten using crimping pliers. Make sure the stop ring is properly seated in its groove and install a new circlip in the groove at the end of the shaft.

Pack the CV-joint and boot with the remaining grease supplied with the boot kit. Peel back the boot and engage the CV-joint inner race splines with the splines on the shaft. Tap the end of the stub shaft with a plastic mallet until the circlip locks in the groove in the CV-joint inner race.

Install the boot over the CV-joint and position it in the groove on the outer race. If the boot is collapsed, insert a dulled screwdriver between the outer race and the boot to admit air or release trapped air from the boot. Smooth out any dimples in the boot with your fingers. Install the large boot clamp and tighten using crimping pliers.

Tripod-Type CV-Joint

NOTE: *The following describes a generalized procedure. Always consult the vehicle service manual for specific instructions.*

Secure the interconnecting shaft in a vise with soft jaw covers. Mark the location of the small end of the boot on the shaft for assembly reference. Use side cutter to cut the large boot clamp and remove the clamp from the boot. Roll the boot back over the shaft.

Slide the tripod housing from the tripod, bending the retaining tabs or prying the retaining ring

out of the way, if required. If necessary, wrap tape around the tripod rollers to keep them and the needle bearings from coming off. Using snapring pliers, move the tripod retaining ring back on the shaft to gain access to the circlip. Remove the circlip and remove the tripod from the shaft.

Disassemble the tripod, if possible. Clean all parts in solvent. Inspect all components for excessive wear, pitting, spalling, looseness, cracking and corrosion. If any components fail inspection, the joint must be replaced.

Install a new boot on the shaft. Position the end of the boot in the groove or in the position marked prior to disassembly. Install a new clamp and tighten using crimping pliers. Install the tripod assembly with the cham-

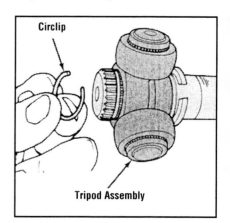

Installing a new circlip on the interconnecting shaft to retain the tripod assembly. *(Courtesy: Ford Motor Co.)*

fered side toward the stop ring.

Install a new circlip on the shaft. Compress the circlip and slide the tripod forward over the circlip to access the stop ring groove. Install the stop ring in the groove with snapring pliers.

Pack the CV-joint and boot with the grease from the boot kit. Install the tripod housing over the tripod. Bend the retaining tabs back in position, if equipped.

Install the boot over the CV-joint and position it in the groove on the tripod housing. If the boot is collapsed, insert a dulled

race, then pull the cage and inner race from the outer race. Pivot the inner race until it is straight up and down in the cage. Align one of the inner race lands with one of the elongated windows and position the race through the window, then rotate the inner race up and out of the cage.

Clean all parts in solvent and check for cracked, broken, severely pitted or worn components. Replace the joint if any components fail inspection.

Pack the ball grooves of the inner and outer races with the grease supplied with the boot kit. Assemble the inner race, cage, outer race and balls in the reverse order of removal, aligning the marks made prior to disassembly. The chamfer in the inner race must face upward screwdriver between the outer race and the boot to admit or release air from the boot. Smooth out any dimples in the boot with your fingers. Install the large boot clamp and tighten using crimping pliers.

Front-Wheel Drive Wheel Bearings

NOTE: The following descriptions are of typical procedures. However, due to the variety of suspension and wheel bearing designs, always consult the service manual for specific procedures and specifications.

Non-Integral Hub And Bearing

With the wheels on the ground, loosen the hub retainer nut. Raise and safely support the vehicle. Remove the wheel and remove and discard the hub retainer nut.

Disconnect the tie-rod end from the steering knuckle and remove the disc brake caliper. Support the caliper out of the way with wire; do not let the caliper hang from the brake hose.

Support the suspension so that tension is removed from the ball joint(s). Support the steering knuckle and separate it from the lower ball joint. Separate the knuckle from the upper ball joint or strut. On some strut vehicles, the strut-to-knuckle bolts also are used for camber adjustment. In this case, mark the position of the fasteners or the strut in the knuckle so that the camber setting will be the same after installation.

Pull outward on the steering knuckle while pulling the halfshaft stub shaft from the hub. If the stub shaft will not pull free, do not hammer on the stub shaft, but use a suitable puller to remove the shaft from the hub. Do not allow the halfshaft to hang unsupported. If necessary, wire it up to keep it from hanging.

Using a suitable prybar, pry the grease seal from the steering knuckle. Using a shop press and

suitable fixtures, press the hub from the steering knuckle. Remove the snapring from the steering knuckle and using a suitable puller, remove the wheel bearing from the knuckle.

Using a shop press and suitable fixtures, press the wheel bearing into the steering knuckle. Press on the outer race of the bearing during installation. Install the snapring.

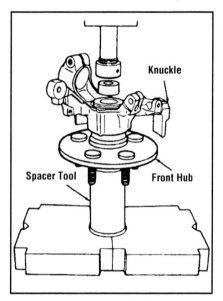

Pressing a wheel hub into the wheel bearing and steering knuckle using a press and suitable fixtures.

Lubricate the lip of a new grease seal with grease and install using a seal installer. Using a shop press and suitable fixtures, press the hub into the steering knuckle. Support the inner bearing race as the hub is pressed in.

Lubricate the splines of the outer CV-joint stub shaft with grease. Install the outboard CV-joint stub shaft into the hub. If the stub shaft will not seat in the hub, use a suitable puller tool to draw it into place; do not use the hub retainer nut.

Connect the lower ball joint to the steering knuckle. Connect the upper ball joint or position the knuckle in the strut, aligning the marks made at removal.

Connect the tie-rod end. Install the brake caliper. Install the wheel and install a new hub retainer nut.

Lower the vehicle. Torque the hub retainer nut to specification. On some vehicles the nut must be staked in place with a dull chisel.

Integral Hub And Bearing

With the wheels on the ground, loosen the hub retainer nut. Raise and safely support the vehicle. Remove the wheel and remove and discard the hub retainer nut.

Remove the disc brake caliper. Support the caliper out of the way with wire; do not let the caliper hang from the brake hose. Remove the disc brake rotor from the hub.

Remove the hub and bearing assembly mounting bolts. Pull the hub and bearing assembly from the steering knuckle and halfshaft stub shaft. If the hub and bearing assembly will not pull free from the stub shaft, do not hammer on the stub shaft, but use a suitable puller to remove the hub from the shaft.

Lubricate the splines of the outer CV-joint stub shaft with grease. Install the hub and bearing assembly over the stub shaft and onto the steering knuckle. Install the mounting bolts and torque to specification.

Install the brake rotor and brake caliper. Install a new hub retainer nut and the wheel. Lower the vehicle. Torque the hub retainer nut to specification.

NOTES

REAR-WHEEL DRIVE AXLE DIAGNOSIS AND REPAIR

DESCRIPTION AND OPERATION

The main purpose of the drive axle is to transfer and multiply torque from the driveshaft to the axle shafts and the wheels. The rotating motion of the driveshaft must be turned 90 degrees and this is accomplished using a hypoid gear set. The hypoid gear set consists of a pinion gear and a ring gear. They are called hypoid because the pinion gear is positioned below the centerline of the ring gear.

Output torque is increased through the gear ratio, which is the ratio between the ring gear teeth and the pinion gear teeth. The ratio is calculated by dividing the number of teeth on the ring gear by the number of teeth on the pinion gear.

The pinion gear rotates on tapered roller bearings in the front of the differential housing. The pinion gear yoke is mounted to the end of the pinion gear, which in turn is attached to the driveshaft. The differential housing can be integral with the drive axle housing or it can be removable. The drive axle housing can be mounted to the frame, as on vehicles with independent rear suspension, or it can be part of a solid axle, which moves up and down with the suspension.

The ring gear is mounted to the differential case, which also rotates on tapered roller bearings, in the differential housing. The differential case contains two side gears and two pinion gears. The pinion gears are bevel gears that rotate on a shaft inside the differential case, called the pinion shaft. The side gears are bevel gears that mesh with the pinion gears and are splined to the ends of the axle shafts.

The axle shafts on a solid drive axle are connected to the wheels. The axle shafts on a vehicle with independent rear suspension are called stub shafts and are connected to halfshafts, which in turn are connected to outer stub shafts and the wheels. Solid axle shafts are called semi floating or full floating, depending on the location of the axle bearings. Semi floating axles have the axle bearings in the axle housing and are used on most cars. Full floating axles have the axle bearings located outside the housing and are used on trucks.

When the vehicle drives straight ahead, the pinion gear turns the ring gear and the differential case. The pinion shaft and gears turn with the case and drive the side gears and the axle shafts. However, when the vehicle turns a corner, the wheel on the outside of the turn must be able to turn faster than the wheel on the inside. To accommodate this, the differential pinion gears can rotate on the pinion shaft, allowing the side gears and axles to turn at different speeds.

The weak point of the conventional differential case design is that when one wheel lacks traction, as when on a patch of ice, the other wheel cannot move the vehicle because power will flow to the wheel that moves easiest. To overcome this deficiency, there are limited slip differentials.

A limited slip differential provides power to both drive wheels at all times. Although there are several designs, the most common type uses clutch packs. The clutch packs contain steel plates and friction discs that are alternately stacked on the differential side gears. The friction plates are splined to the gears and the plates have tabs that lock them in the differential case, so the discs turn with the side gears and the plates turn with the case. A diaphragm spring or a set of coil springs applies pressure to the clutch packs. As a result, both axles turn with the differential case, yet the clutch packs slip enough to allow the vehicle to turn corners.

A cone clutch limited slip differential works similarly to the clutch pack design, except it uses cone-shaped gears to produce friction. A set of coil springs force the cones against the ends of the differential case. The axles are splined to the cone gears and turn with the differential case, but just like the clutch pack differential, the cone gears slip enough for the vehicle to turn corners.

Another type of limited slip differential uses gears rather than friction devices to provide torque to both wheels. A Torsen, or torque-sensing differential has advantages over clutch type units in that it does not bind in turns or lose its effectiveness from wear.

DIAGNOSIS

The most common symptoms of rear axle problems are fluid leaks and noise. The rear axle can leak at the pinion seal, axle seals or at the cover. Pinion and axle seals can leak due to normal wear and age or because of excessive pinion bearing or axle bearing play. The axle can also leak if it is overfilled or if excessive pressure builds up due to a clogged axle vent.

Drive axle noise can be difficult to diagnose because other vehicle systems and components can produce similar noises. Bad tires, bent wheels, worn U-joints, worn wheel bearings, worn transmission gears or bearings, and even suspension and exhaust system components can all create noise that may sound like it's coming from the rear axle. Road test the vehicle and try to narrow down the conditions during which the noise occurs: under acceleration, deceleration, at cruise or when

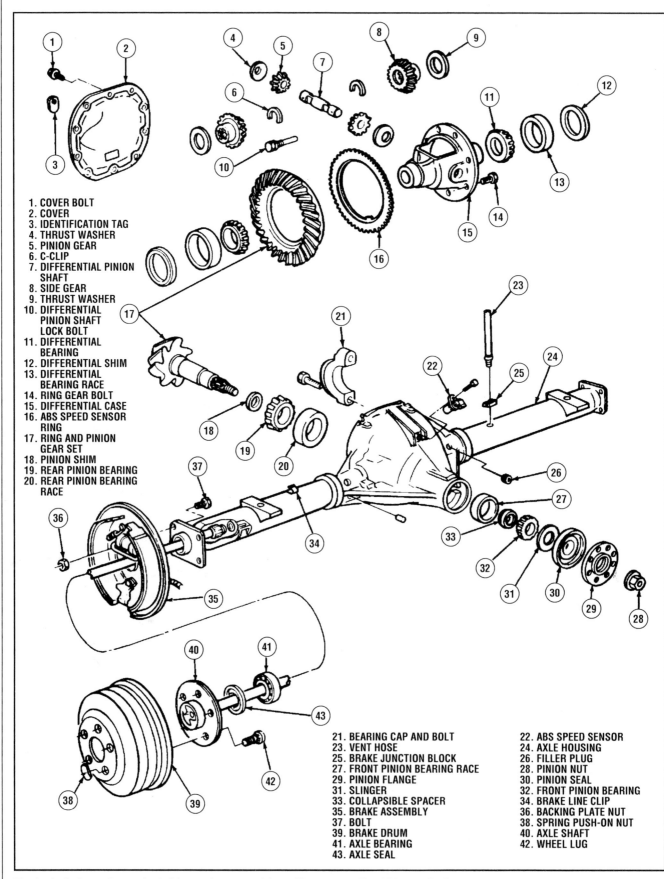

1. COVER BOLT
2. COVER
3. IDENTIFICATION TAG
4. THRUST WASHER
5. PINION GEAR
6. C-CLIP
7. DIFFERENTIAL PINION SHAFT
8. SIDE GEAR
9. THRUST WASHER
10. DIFFERENTIAL PINION SHAFT LOCK BOLT
11. DIFFERENTIAL BEARING
12. DIFFERENTIAL SHIM
13. DIFFERENTIAL BEARING RACE
14. RING GEAR BOLT
15. DIFFERENTIAL CASE
16. ABS SPEED SENSOR RING
17. RING AND PINION GEAR SET
18. PINION SHIM
19. REAR PINION BEARING
20. REAR PINION BEARING RACE

21. BEARING CAP AND BOLT
23. VENT HOSE
25. BRAKE JUNCTION BLOCK
27. FRONT PINION BEARING RACE
29. PINION FLANGE
31. SLINGER
33. COLLAPSIBLE SPACER
35. BRAKE ASSEMBLY
37. BOLT
39. BRAKE DRUM
41. AXLE BEARING
43. AXLE SEAL

22. ABS SPEED SENSOR
24. AXLE HOUSING
26. FILLER PLUG
28. PINION NUT
30. PINION SEAL
32. FRONT PINION BEARING
34. BRAKE LINE CLIP
36. BACKING PLATE NUT
38. SPRING PUSH-ON NUT
40. AXLE SHAFT
42. WHEEL LUG

Exploded view of a typical drive axle assembly.   (Courtesy: Ford Motor Co.)

going around turns.

If the same noise persists during both acceleration and deceleration conditions, then the noise is probably coming from another part of the car such as the tires, front-wheel bearings or the U-joints. If the noise changes with the type of road being driven on, then the sound is probably tire noise or plain old road noise. If you hear the same noise or a similar noise while driving and sitting, it must be coming from the engine or clutch assembly. Rear axle noise doesn't change with the type of road surface. Unlike the differential, tire noise doesn't change under acceleration and deceleration conditions.

Whining or howling noises are usually gear related and will change when the vehicle accelerates and decelerates. Whining can be caused by an improperly set gear tooth contact pattern or a gear pattern that has changed due to improper bearing preload. Howling can be caused by excessive runout of the ring gear, differential case or pinion gear.

A growling sound may be caused by differential, pinion or axle bearings. This noise is usually constant, however, a faulty front or rear pinion bearing may be isolated by whether the noise changes during acceleration to deceleration. Axle shaft bearing noise can be verified by steering left and right while driving, rocking the vehicle to move the weight more right and left. Bearing noise that is noticeably worse in one direction indicates that the opposite axle shaft bearing is at fault.

Problems inside the differential case can also become evident when turning corners. Damaged side gears and/or pinion gears can make a clunking sound and sticking clutch packs in a limited slip differential can make a chattering sound. Sticking clutch packs can be caused by incorrect lubricant and many manufacturers specify that a special lubricant additive be used for this problem.

If there is a clunking noise on acceleration and sometimes on deceleration, and you have eliminated the universal joints as the source of the problem, suspect the differential pinion shaft. A clunking noise can also be caused by excessive backlash between the ring and pinion.

DRIVE AXLE SERVICE

Pinion Seal Replacement

Raise and safely support the vehicle. Remove the wheels. Remove the brake drums or rotors to prevent drag when adjusting the pinion bearing preload.

Mark the position of the rear U-joint or yoke on the differential pinion flange or yoke, for assembly reference, and then remove the driveshaft.

Install an inch pound torque wrench and socket on the pinion nut and record the torque required to maintain rotation of the pinion through several revolutions.

Hold the differential pinion yoke or flange and remove the pinion nut. Clean the area around the pinion seal and place a drain pan under the seal. Mark the flange or yoke in relation to the pinion shaft, for assembly reference. Remove the flange or yoke from the pinion shaft, using a puller.

CAUTION: Never strike the pinion flange or yoke with a hammer in an attempt to remove it from the pinion shaft.

Remove the pinion seal using a puller or seal removal tool. Clean the oil seal seat surface in the differential housing. Install a new seal with a suitable seal installer. Coat the lips of the new seal with grease.

Inspect the pinion flange or yoke splines and seal mating surface for burrs, wear or other damage. Replace if any defects are found. Lubricate the pinion flange or yoke splines and install it on the pinion shaft, aligning the marks made at removal. Lubricate the washer side of a new pinion nut and install the

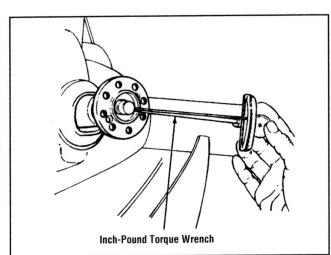

Measuring pinion bearing torque preload using an inch pound torque wrench. *(Courtesy: Ford Motor Co.)*

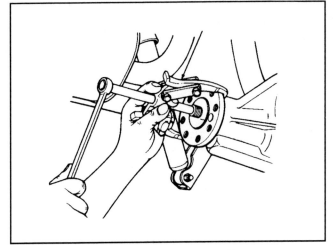

Removing the pinion flange using a puller. *(Courtesy: Ford Motor Co.)*

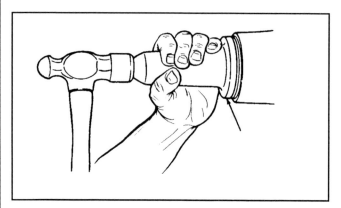

Installing a new pinion seal.
(Courtesy: Ford Motor Co.)

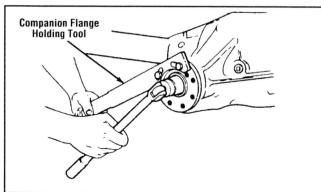

Hold the pinion flange while tightening the pinion nut.
(Courtesy: Ford Motor Co.)

nut on the pinion shaft. Hold the pinion flange or yoke and tighten the pinion nut.

Rotate the pinion shaft occasionally while tightening the nut, and take frequent pinion bearing torque preload readings until the original recorded preload is obtained. Refer to the vehicle service manual to see if additional torque is required.

Install the driveshaft, aligning the marks made at removal. Install the brake drums or rotors and install the wheels. Check the fluid level in the differential and add fluid if necessary. Lower the vehicle.

Ring And Pinion Removal And Installation

Raise and safely support the vehicle. Remove the wheels and the brake drums or rotors. Mark the position of the rear U-joint or yoke on the differential pinion flange or yoke, for assembly reference, and then remove the driveshaft.

If the axle shafts are retained at the ends of the axle tubes, remove the retaining nuts and pull the axle shafts from the axle housing. It may be necessary to use a slide hammer to remove the axle shafts.

If the axle shafts are retained with C-clips, clean the area around the differential housing cover and position a drain pan under the cover. Loosen the cover bolts and drain the fluid from the differential, then remove the cover. Rotate the differential case until the differential case pinion shaft lock bolt is accessible. Remove the lock bolt and slide the pinion shaft out of the case.

Push the axle shafts in enough to access the C-clips. Remove the C-clips and the axle shafts. Reinstall the pinion shaft and lock bolt once the axle shafts are removed.

If the differential carrier is removable, clean the area where the carrier mates to the axle housing, then position a drain pan under the carrier and loosen the carrier retaining nuts. Pull the carrier away from the drive axle housing and drain the fluid. Remove the retaining nuts and remove the differential carrier from the axle housing. Secure the differential carrier on a workbench.

Before removing the differential case from the carrier, check for ring gear runout using a dial indicator. If runout is beyond specification, the differential case

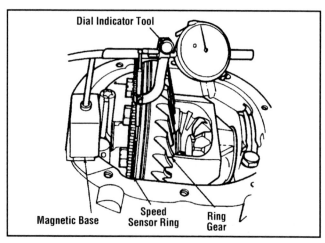

Checking ring gear runout with a dial indicator prior to disassembly. *(Courtesy: Ford Motor Co.)*

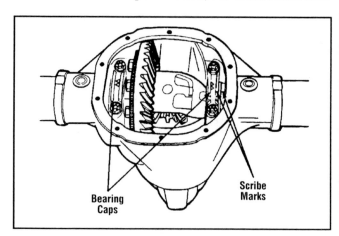

Mark the location of the differential bearing caps so they can be reinstalled properly.
(Courtesy: Ford Motor Co.)

runout will need to be checked before a new ring gear is installed.

Mark the position of the differential bearing caps so they can be reinstalled in their original locations. If equipped with threaded bearing adjusters, remove the lock retaining bolts and locks from the bearing caps, loosen the bearing cap bolts and back off the adjusters. Remove the bearing cap bolts and the bearing caps. Lift the differential case, bearing races and adjusters from the differential housing. Keep the adjusters and bearing races with their respective differential bearings.

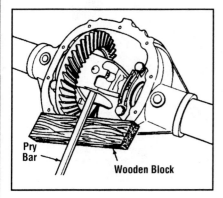

Removing the differential case from the differential carrier.
(Courtesy: Ford Motor Co.)

If differential bearing preload and backlash is adjusted with shims, the differential case will usually need to be pried out of the carrier. Loosen the bearing cap bolts and caps. Position a wood block on the carrier, below the case, to protect the carrier face. Position a pry bar in the case opening and pry out until the case, bearing races and shims are loose in the bearing caps. Remove the bearing caps and the differential case from the carrier.

Hold the differential pinion yoke or flange with a suitable tool and remove the pinion nut. Clean the area around the pinion seal. If the pinion gear is to be reused, mark the flange or yoke in relation to the pinion shaft, for

assembly reference. Remove the flange or yoke from the pinion shaft, using a puller.

CAUTION: Never strike the pinion flange or yoke with a hammer in an attempt to remove it from the pinion shaft.

Remove the pinion seal using a puller or seal removal tool. Drive the pinion out of the front pinion bearing using a soft mallet and remove the pinion through the rear of the carrier. Remove the collapsible spacer from the pinion shaft and remove the front pinion bearing from the carrier.

Remove the differential case pinion shaft lock bolt and slide the pinion shaft from the case. Rotate the differential case side gears until the pinion gears can be removed from the opening in the case. Remove the pinion gears, side gears and washers. Keep track of the orientation of the gears and washers so they can be reinstalled in their original locations. (For inspection of limited slip differential components, please refer to the Limited Slip Differential section in this study guide.)

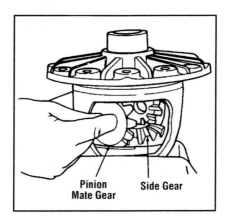

Removing the pinion gears from the differential case.
(Courtesy: Ford Motor Co.)

Thoroughly clean the pinion and ring gears, differential case and differential case pinion shaft, side gears, pinion gears and thrust washers. Examine the ring and pinion gears for cracks,

scoring, galling, broken or chipped teeth and other damage. Inspect the pinion and case bearings and races for cracks, pitting, galling, roughness or other damage. Inspect the differential case and machined surfaces for cracks, wear and other damage. Inspect the differential case side gear and pinion gear teeth for scuffed, nicked, burred or broken teeth. Inspect the thrust washers for wear, nicks and scuffs. A ring and pinion is a matched set and must always be replaced as an assembly. Roller bearings must always be replaced as an assembly with their races.

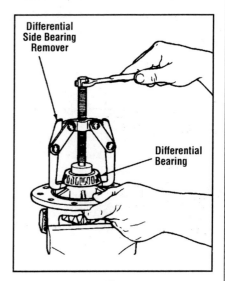

Removing the differential bearings from the differential case.
(Courtesy: Ford Motor Co.)

If bearing replacement is necessary, remove the differential bearings from the case using a suitable puller and press new bearings into position. Remove the pinion bearing races from the differential carrier by striking them alternately on opposite sides with a suitable drift. Be careful not to damage the bores in the carrier. Install new races using a suitable installer. Use a suitable press fixture under the rear pinion bearing and press the bearing from the pinion shaft. Save the shim that is found under the bearing.

If the ring and pinion are being

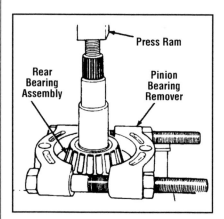

Removing the rear pinion bearing from the pinion shaft.
(Courtesy: Ford Motor Co.)

replaced, remove the ring gear bolts from the differential case. Remove the ring gear from the case using a drift that will fit into the bottom of the ring gear bolt holes without contacting and damaging the threads. Strike at alternate holes around the ring gear until it is free of the case. Support the ring gear as it comes loose.

If the ring gear runout was excessive when checked prior to disassembly, reinstall the differential case in the carrier and set the bearing preload. Check the case runout using a dial indicator. If runout exceeds specifications and new case bearings have not been installed, remove the differential case. Install new bearings and races, reinstall the case and set the bearing preload, then recheck case runout. If runout is still excessive, the differential case must be replaced.

Install the pinion and side gears in the differential case with the thrust washers. Check side gear end-play using a dial indicator and correct using different thickness thrust washers if end-play is not within specification. After end-play adjustment, install the cross differential pin and the lock pin bolt.

Examine the new ring and pinion for markings indicating that they are a matched set, the gear ratio, timing marks and pinion depth. If the gear ratio is being changed, make sure the new gears are compatible with the differential case. When changing to some gear ratios, the case must also be changed.

Timing marks indicate that those ring and pinion gear teeth must be meshed when installed. There are hunting type gear sets and non-hunting type gear sets. Hunting gear sets, where any one pinion gear tooth contacts all ring gear teeth, are not marked and can be installed in any mesh position. On non-hunting type gear sets, where any one pinion gear tooth contacts only a certain number of teeth, the marks on the ring and pinion gear must be aligned when they are installed.

Pinion depth is the distance from the face of the pinion gear to the centerline of the ring gear. This figure may be marked on the pinion gear or there may be plus or minus numbers, indicating how many thousandths of an inch must be added or subtracted from the pinion depth measurement.

Before installing the new ring gear, examine the differential case flange and the ring gear mating surface for burrs or any other irregularities that could prevent the ring gear from seating properly and possibly cause excessive runout. Use a file or stone to eliminate any imperfections. Install the ring gear using new ring gear bolts. Tighten the bolts, drawing the ring gear against the differential case flange gradually and evenly. Torque the bolts to specification.

Before the pinion gear can be installed, the pinion depth must be set. Pinion depth is controlled by the thickness of a shim or shims, usually located between the rear pinion bearing and the pinion gear. If the original ring and pinion, pinion bearings and differential case are being reused, then the original shim(s) can also be reused. However, if any of the aforementioned components are replaced, then the pinion depth must be measured and adjusted as necessary.

Pinion depth is set using a special gauge fixture. The front and rear pinion bearings are installed in their races and held in place with special plates and a clamp screw. The fixture is positioned

Measuring pinion depth.   *(Courtesy: GM Corp.)*

in the differential bearing saddles and a dial indicator and extension measures the distance to the gauge plate. The shim thickness that is needed is the difference between the measured pinion depth and the specified depth.

Place the pinion shim(s) over the pinion shaft and press on the rear pinion bearing. Lubricate the front pinion bearing and install it in the differential carrier. Install a new pinion seal. Install a new collapsible spacer over the pinion gear shaft, lubricate the rear pinion bearing with gear oil and install the pinion gear in the differential carrier.

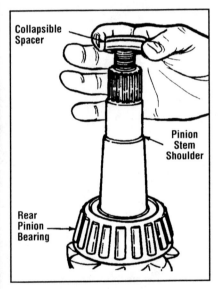

Installing a new collapsible spacer on the pinion gear shaft.
(Courtesy: Ford Motor Co.)

Lubricate the pinion shaft and yoke or flange splines. If the original pinion and yoke or flange are being reused, align the marks made before disassembly. Install the yoke or flange on the pinion shaft and install a new pinion nut. Hold the yoke or flange with a suitable tool and tighten the pinion nut. Rotate the pinion frequently to make sure the bearings seat properly. Measure the bearing torque preload frequently with an inch pound torque wrench. Tighten the pinion nut until the specified

preload is obtained. In general, the preload torque for used bearings will be less than for new bearings.

If backlash and differential bearing preload are adjusted with threaded adjusters, lubricate the differential case bearings and adjuster threads with gear oil and place the bearings races over the bearings. Install the differential case with the bearings races and adjusters. If there were timing marks on the ring and pinion, make sure these align. Position the case and adjusters so there is some backlash and then install the bearing caps. Make sure the bearing caps and adjusters are installed in their original locations, as marked before removal.

Tighten the bearing cap bolts, while making sure the threaded adjusters can turn easily. Torque the bearing cap bolts to specification, then back off the bolts enough to allow the adjusters to be turned. Loosen the right side adjuster, and then tighten the left side adjuster, while rotating the ring gear, until there is no backlash. Torque the left side bearing cap to specification. Tighten the right side adjuster until there is no side play in the differential case bearings.

Position a dial indicator to check backlash. Torque the right side bearing cap bolts to specification, then turn the right side adjuster until the correct backlash and bearing preload is obtained. Check the backlash at several points around the ring gear. If backlash is not as specified, turn each adjuster equal amounts in the necessary direction, to obtain the correct backlash while maintaining bearing preload. Be sure to install the adjuster locks in the bearing caps once backlash and preload adjustments are finalized.

If backlash and differential bearing preload are adjusted with shims, lubricate the differential case bearings with gear oil and place the bearings races over the bearings. If the original case

Adjusting ring gear backlash on a vehicle with threaded adjusters.
(Courtesy: DaimlerChrysler Corp.)

and bearings are being reused, then the original shims can be used. However, if a new case or bearings are being installed, shims of different thickness will be necessary. Initially, try to select shim sets that will allow some backlash and at the same time eliminate differential bearing side play. Install the differential case with the bearings races and shims. If there were timing marks on the ring and pinion, make sure these align.

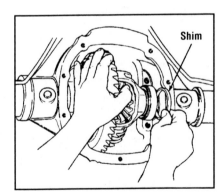

Installing a differential carrier bearing shim.
(Courtesy: Ford Motor Co.)

Install the bearing caps, making sure they are installed in their original locations, and tighten the cap bolts to specification. Position a dial indicator and check backlash. Check the backlash at several points around the ring gear. Add shim thickness from one side and remove an equal amount from the other side until backlash is correct and zero side play is maintained. Once the correct backlash is obtained, add equal amounts of shim thickness to each side, to obtain the bearing preload specified by the manufacturer.

The accuracy of the pinion depth setting is verified by checking the tooth contact pattern. Apply contact pattern checking compound to the drive and coast sides of the ring gear teeth. To obtain the drive side pattern, turn the pinion gear with a wrench, in the normal direction of rotation, while applying a drag to the ring gear. To obtain the coast side pattern, turn the pinion in the opposite direction.

Examine the gear tooth contact pattern. A correct drive side pattern will be centered in the tooth. The length of the pattern at the top of the tooth will be approximately the same as the length at the root, and the pattern will be square at the heel and toe. The coast side pattern should be approximately the same as the drive side. If the drive side pattern is located toward the top of the tooth, with the length of the pattern longer at the top than at the root, the pinion is too shallow and needs to be shimmed toward the ring gear. If the drive side pattern is located toward the root of the tooth, with the length of the pattern longer at the root than at the top, the pinion is too deep and must be shimmed away from the ring gear.

If the drive side pattern is located toward the heel, the backlash is excessive and the ring gear must be moved towards the pinion. If the drive side pattern is located toward the toe, the backlash is insufficient and the ring gear must be moved away from the pinion.

Make corrections as required. Move the ring gear or pinion in small amounts in the necessary direction and recheck the pattern. Whenever the pinion is removed and reinstalled, a new collapsible spacer must be used.

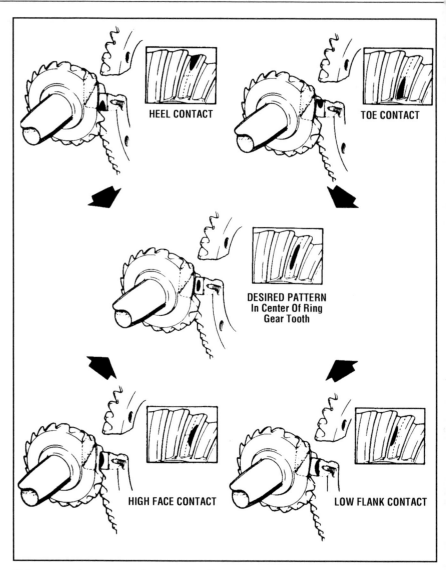

Drive side ring and pinion gear tooth contact patterns. *(Courtesy: GM Corp.)*

Install a removable carrier to the drive axle housing, using a new gasket, and torque the nuts to specification. Install the axle shafts. Torque the differential case pinion shaft lock bolt to specification. On integral carriers, install the differential cover using a new gasket. Install the driveshaft, aligning the marks made prior to removal.

Remove the filler plug and fill the differential carrier with the proper type of lubricant until it begins to come out the filler plug hole. Consult the vehicle service manual to see if a limited slip additive should be used. Install the filler plug.

Install the brake drums or rotors and the wheels. Lower the vehicle and road test.

Limited Slip Differential

NOTE: *The following information applies to clutch pack-type limited slip differentials.*

The operation of the limited slip differential can be checked by measuring the torque required to turn one wheel while the other is held. Raise one wheel off the ground. Attach a suitable adapter that goes over

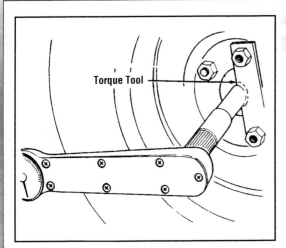

Checking limited slip differential operation.
(Courtesy: Ford Motor Co.)

the lug nuts and provides for torque wrench attachment. Place the transmission in neutral. Turn the wheel with a torque wrench and note the reading when the wheel begins to turn. The reading when the wheel begins to turn is the break-away torque, and may be higher than the continuous turning torque.

Compare the break-away torque reading to specification. If the torque reading is lower than speci-

fication, the clutch packs or preload springs are probably worn.

If service is required, remove the differential case as described under Ring and Pinion Replacement. Remove the ring gear bolts from the differential case. Mark the position of the ring gear on the differential case prior to removal. Remove the ring gear from the case using a drift that will fit into the bottom of the ring gear bolt holes without contacting and damaging the threads. Strike at alternate holes around the ring gear until it is free of the case. Support the ring gear as it comes loose. The differential case bearings need not be removed unless they are damaged.

Remove the pinion shaft and the preload spring assembly. Use a suitable tool to rotate the case or pinion gears so the pinion gears can be removed from the case opening. When the pinion gears are accessible, remove them and

their thrust washers from the case. Remove the clutch packs, shims and side gears from the case. Keep track of all components so, if reused, they can be reinstalled in their original locations.

Clean and inspect the clutch pack plates and friction discs. Replace parts as necessary. Lubricate the plates and friction discs with limited slip differential lubricant and assemble the clutch pack without the shims.

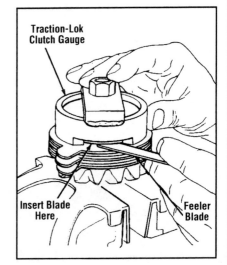

Determining clutch pack shim thickness with a gauge tool and feeler gauge.
(Courtesy: Ford Motor Co.)

The method for determining shim thickness varies depending on manufacturer. The clutch packs may be assembled in a special gauge tool and the shim thickness determined by feeler gauge, or the packs may be installed in the case with the side and pinion gears and shim thickness determined by pinion tooth clearance using a dial indicator. Refer to the vehicle service manual for specific instructions.

Install the clutch packs, shims and side gears in the differential case. Rotate the pinion gears into position. Install the preload spring assembly and the pinion gear shaft. Install the pinion shaft lock bolt.

There are special tools that can allow the differential to be tested

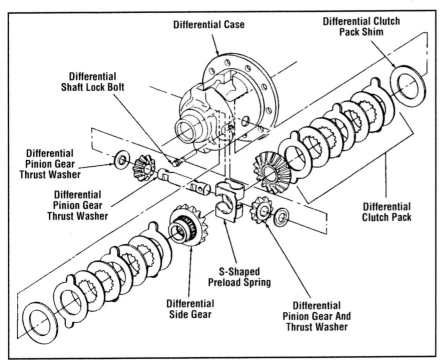

Exploded view of a typical clutch pack-type limited slip differential assembly.
(Courtesy: Ford Motor Co.)

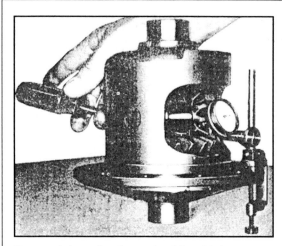

Determining clutch pack shim thickness by measuring pinion gear tooth clearance with a dial indicator. *(Courtesy: GM Corp.)*

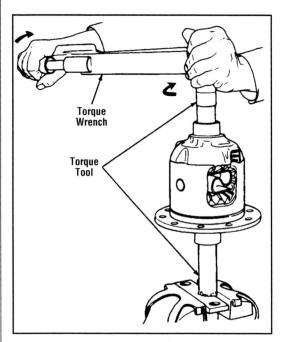

Bench testing a limited slip differential. *(Courtesy: Ford Motor Co.)*

before it is reinstalled in the vehicle. The test is similar to the limited slip operation test that can be performed with the differential installed in the vehicle.

Install the ring gear on the differential case and install the differential in the vehicle.

Axle Shafts

Wheel Studs

Raise and safely support the vehicle. Remove the brake drum or the brake rotor. Inspect for stripped threads and loose or broken studs.

Remove the stud(s) using a suitable press fixture. Inspect the hole in the axle shaft after the stud is removed. If the hole is elongated or distorted, the axle shaft must be replaced.

Draw the new stud into position using a nut and several washers. Make sure the head of the stud is completely seated on the axle shaft flange.

Install the brake drum or rotor. Install the wheel and torque the lug nuts to specification. Lower the vehicle.

Axle Shafts, Bearings And Seals

Raise and safely support the vehicle. Remove the wheels and the brake drums or rotors.

If the axle shafts are retained at the ends of the axle tubes, remove the retaining nuts and pull the axle shafts from the axle housing. It may be necessary to use a slide hammer to remove the axle shafts. Use a puller or seal removal tool to remove the axle seal from the axle housing.

If the axle shafts are retained with C-clips, clean the area around the differential housing cover and position a drain pan under the cover. Loosen the cover bolts and drain the fluid from the differential, then remove the cover. Rotate the differential case until the differential case pinion shaft lock bolt is accessible. Remove the lock bolt and slide the pinion

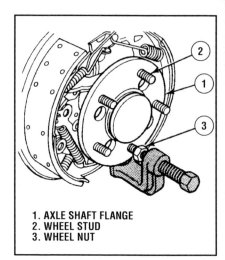

1. AXLE SHAFT FLANGE
2. WHEEL STUD
3. WHEEL NUT

Removing a wheel stud from an axle shaft. *(Courtesy: GM Corp.)*

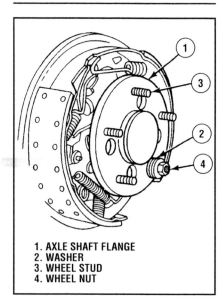

1. AXLE SHAFT FLANGE
2. WASHER
3. WHEEL STUD
4. WHEEL NUT

Installing a wheel stud in an axle shaft. *(Courtesy: GM Corp.)*

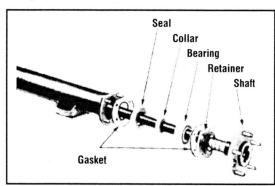

Exploded view of an axle shaft, bearing and seal assembly with a retainer plate.

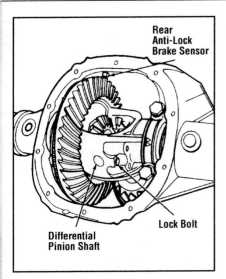

Differential pinion shaft and lock bolt location.
(Courtesy: Ford Motor Co.)

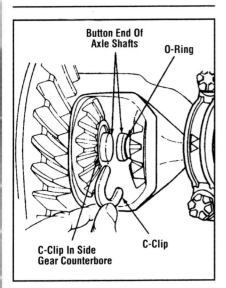

Removing the C-clip from the end of the axle shaft.
(Courtesy: Ford Motor Co.)

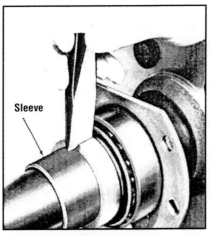

Using a chisel to remove the axle bearing retaining ring.
(Courtesy: DaimlerChrysler Corp.)

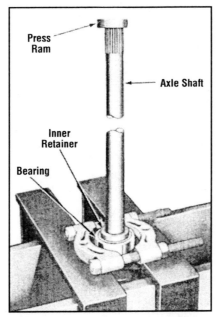

Pressing the axle bearing from the axle shaft.
(Courtesy: Ford Motor Co.)

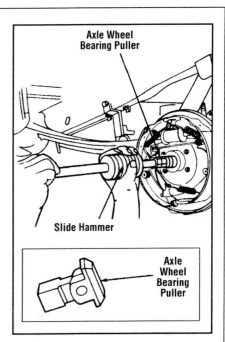

Removing the axle shaft bearing using a puller and slide hammer.
(Courtesy: Ford Motor Co.)

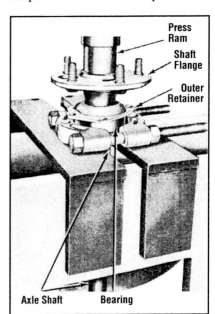

Pressing a new bearing onto the axle shaft.
(Courtesy: Ford Motor Co.)

shaft out of the case. Push the axle shafts in enough to access the C-clips. Remove the C-clips and the axle shafts. Reinstall the pinion shaft and lock bolt once the axle shafts are removed.

Axle shafts with retainer plates use bearings that are pressed onto the shaft. A retaining ring is used to help secure the bearing to the shaft and this ring must be removed before the old bearing can be pressed off. Grind a notch in the retaining ring and use a chisel to split it, then remove the retaining ring from the axle.

Position the axle shaft in a press, with a press plate fixture under the bearing. The press plate should be positioned so it contacts the inner bearing race. Press the bearing off of the shaft.

Axle shafts that use C-clips are supported by bearings that are pressed into the axle housing. Use a seal removal tool or puller to remove the axle seal, then use a puller and slide hammer to remove the axle bearing from the housing.

Inspect the axle shaft bearings for pitting, galling, spalling, brinelling, roughness or other damage. Replace bearings as required. Inspect the axle shaft splines for wear and damage and inspect the seal contact area for damage. Replace axles that are damaged.

To press on a new axle shaft bearing, install the retainer plate, oil seal, if equipped, and bearing onto the axle shaft. Position the axle shaft in a press. Press the bearing onto the shaft, making sure the bearing is supported on the inner race. Remove the axle shaft from the press and install a new retaining ring. Reposition the axle shaft in the press. Press the retaining ring onto the shaft, making sure the retaining ring is properly supported.

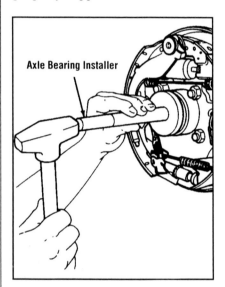

Axle Bearing Installer

Installing a new axle shaft bearing into the axle housing.
(Courtesy: Ford Motor Co.)

Press a new axle shaft seal into the axle housing and lubricate the lips of the seal with gear lubricant. Lubricate the axle shaft splines and install the axle shaft with a new gasket. Align the axle shaft splines with the differential side gear splines and slide the axle shaft into position. Install the retaining nuts and torque to specification. Check the axle shaft end-play using a dial indicator. End-play that is not within specification is usually changed with shims, but refer to the vehicle service manual for specific instructions.

On C-clip axles, lubricate a new bearing with gear lubricant and install it in the axle housing using a suitable driver. Install a new axle shaft seal and lubricate the lips of the seal with gear lubricant. Lubricate the axle shaft splines, align the splines with the differential side gear splines and slide the axle shaft into position.

Install the C-clip on the end of the axle shaft and then pull the axle shaft outward until the C-clip seats in the recess in the differential side gear. Install the differential pinion shaft. Apply threadlocking compound to the pinion shaft lock bolt and install the lock bolt through the differential case and into the pinion shaft. Torque the pinion shaft lock bolt to specification.

Install the differential housing cover with a new gasket. Remove the filler plug and fill the differential carrier with the proper type of lubricant until it begins to come out the filler plug hole. Consult the vehicle service manual to see if a limited slip additive should be used. Install the filler plug.

Install the brake drums or rotors and the wheels. Lower the vehicle.

NOTES

FOUR-WHEEL DRIVE/ALL-WHEEL DRIVE COMPONENT DIAGNOSIS AND REPAIR

DESCRIPTION AND OPERATION

Four-Wheel Drive (4WD) and All-Wheel Drive (AWD) systems supply power to both the front and rear wheels of a vehicle, for increased traction and vehicle control in rain, snow and off-road driving.

4WD systems can be part time or full time. On a part time system, the driver can shift into 4WD when it is needed, but for normal driving conditions the vehicle can be operated as a conventional rear-wheel drive vehicle. Part time 4WD is usually used in trucks and SUVs. Vehicles with full time 4WD and AWD operate in 4WD at all times.

Although many manufacturers use the terms interchangeably, in general 4WD refers to systems that use a separate transfer case. AWD vehicles usually do not have a transfer case and are usually based on a front-wheel drive vehicle. The transaxle in an AWD vehicle uses a viscous clutch or center differential, which transfers power to a driveshaft and rear drive axle.

The transfer case in a 4WD system is attached to or driven by a shaft from the vehicle's transmission. Output shafts in the transfer case turn driveshafts that are connected to differentials on the front and rear axles.

A typical part time 4WD transfer case operates in 2H (two-wheel high), 4H (four-wheel high) and 4L (four-wheel low). Under normal driving conditions the transfer case will operate in 2H and power will be transferred to the rear driveshaft only. 4H is activated either by moving a shifter with mechanical linkage that moves a shift fork in the transfer case, or by a switch that activates an electric or vacuum motor, which in turn moves the shift fork. In 4H, power is transferred to both the front and rear

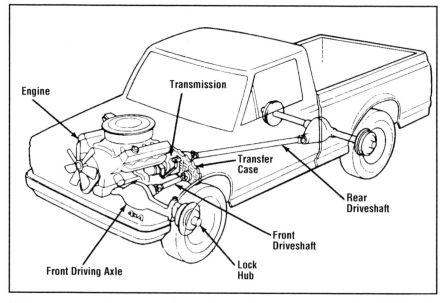

Major components of a part-time 4WD system.
(Courtesy: Ford Motor Co.)

driveshafts. Shifting from 2H to 4H can be done while the vehicle is moving or when it is stopped. 4L provides further gear reduction and pulling power. Low range can generally only be activated when the vehicle is stopped or moving very slowly.

The front wheels can be engaged and disengaged from the front driveline on vehicles with part time 4WD. This is necessary because just as there is a speed difference between the inside and outside wheels of an axle on a turn, there are speed differences between the front and rear wheels. The differential handles the speed difference on an axle, but on a part time 4WD vehicle, the front wheels are not free to turn independently of the rear wheels when in 4WD and for this reason vehicles with part time 4WD should not be operated on dry pavement in 4WD. There is no problem on dirt or snow because these surfaces will allow the wheels to slip, but on a dry surface there will be torsional windup due to one driveline com-

ponent traveling farther than another.

There are several ways to lock and unlock the front wheels to the drivetrain. Older part time 4WD vehicles used manual or automatic locking hubs. Manual locking hubs are engaged by turning a dial in the center of the hub. When manual locking hubs are engaged, the front driveshaft, differential and axle shafts will turn regardless of whether or not the transfer case is in 4WD. Automatic locking hubs are engaged by one way clutches in the hubs. The hubs lock when the transfer case is in 4WD and the front axles are being turned. They disengage when the transfer case is shifted out of 4WD or on some vehicles, by backing up a certain distance.

Most newer vehicles use an axle disconnect mechanism activated by a vacuum or electric motor. The vacuum motor or electric motor is located on the axle assembly and is engaged when the transfer case is shifted to 4WD. When the motor is

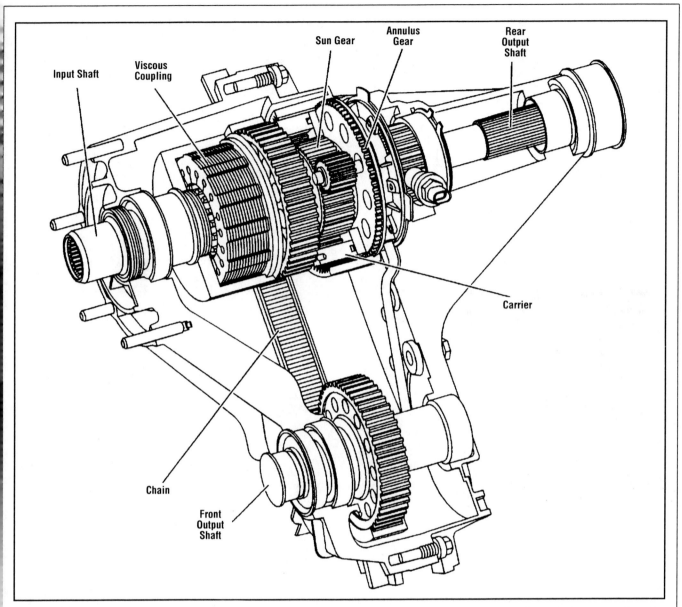

Cutaway view of a fulltime 4WD transfer case. This transfer case utilizes a planetary differential gear and a viscous coupling to divide the torque between the front and rear wheels.
(Courtesy: GM Corp.)

engaged, it moves a collar that connects one of the axle shafts to the front differential for 4WD operation.

When a vehicle with part time 4WD is operated in rear-wheel drive only and the wheels are not engaged, the front wheels can freewheel and certain components of the front driveline do not turn. This improves fuel economy and saves unnecessary wear on components.

Vehicles with full time 4WD or AWD have a center differential and/or viscous clutch to divide torque between the front and rear axles. These systems are generally not used on vehicles that will be driven off-road, but rather are intended to increase vehicle performance when driving on icy or snowy roads.

During normal operation, the transfer case shown in the illustration delivers 62% of the engine's torque to the rear wheels and 38% to the front. However, if the front wheels begin to slip, more torque is biased toward the rear wheels, which have traction, and less to the front. The opposite occurs if the rear wheels begin to slip. Then, more torque is sent to the front wheels and less to the rear.

DIAGNOSIS

Since 4WD and AWD vehicles share components like driveshafts, halfshafts and differentials with front-wheel drive and rear-wheel drive vehicles, the diagnosis and repair procedures for these components will be the same. Problems that are peculiar to 4WD and AWD vehicles are with the transfer case and wheel locking mechanisms.

The most common transfer case problems are leaks, noise and jumping out of gear. Check all seams for gasket leaks and tighten any loose bolts. If the seals are leaking, inspect the yokes for burrs that may be tearing the sealing surfaces. Excessive lubricant is another cause of leaks, as is a plugged vent. Transfer cases often have remote vents leading up into the engine compartment to keep dirt and water from entering the case.

If the transfer case is noisy, it may be low on lubricant. Other causes of noise include worn or damaged bearings, worn or misaligned driveshafts or universal joints, loose bolts or linkage, and a worn chain.

If the transfer case is hard to shift, inspect the linkage for dirt, mud or stones. If the problem isn't visible, it is probably internal and the transfer case will have to be disassembled for inspection of the gears, bearings and chain. If it won't stay in gear, the linkage may have to be adjusted. Also, check for a bent shift rod; missing detent balls or springs; and worn or damaged gears.

Electronic shift transfer cases may not shift at all when switched on, there may be clicking and chattering without shifting, the shift may not be smooth or the vehicle may have to be stopped to shift (2H-4H), or the shift may occur but the indicator lights may not work. Check for blown fuses and check power sources and grounds, then check the system sensors and the shift motor. If these are OK, check the shift switches.

Manual locking hubs are generally very reliable, however, they can be hard to engage or disengage if water or dirt has gotten inside and jammed or corroded the mechanism. Automatic locking hubs can suffer from the same problems, and since they

are not engaged manually and their internal mechanism is more complicated, there is a greater chance that they will fail. In both cases the hubs must be disassembled and inspected.

Vacuum leaks are the main problems with vacuum motor engagement systems. Check for leaks at the switch, on the transfer case, at the vacuum motor on the axle, and check the vacuum lines. The axle disconnect mechanism can also fail to operate due to worn or failed components.

SERVICE

Transfer Case

Transfer Case Fluid

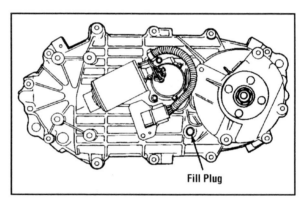

Typical transfer case fill plug location. *(Courtesy: Ford Motor Co.)*

Remove the fill plug from the transfer case. Check the fluid level with your finger; it should be just below the level of the fill plug hole. Top off with the recommended fluid, as necessary, and reinstall the fill plug. Tighten the fill plug to specification.

Make sure that the transfer case is filled with the proper type of fluid. If in doubt as to the type or quality of the fluid, the transfer case fluid should be drained and replaced with the type specified by the vehicle manufacturer.

To change the transfer case fluid, raise and safely support the vehicle, then remove the transfer case drain plug and drain the fluid into a clean container. Inspect the fluid for parti-

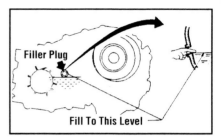

Checking transfer case fluid level. *(Courtesy: Nissan Motor Co., Ltd.)*

cles that could indicate internal problems.

After the fluid has completely drained, reinstall the drain plug using a new gasket, if equipped. Fill the transfer case to the proper level with the specified lubricant.

Oil Seal Replacement

Raise and safely support the vehicle. Mark the position of the driveshaft on the output shaft flange or yoke. Remove the driveshaft from the flange or yoke and wire it up out of the way.

Hold the output shaft yoke or flange with a suitable holding tool and remove the nut retaining the yoke or flange to the output shaft, then remove the yoke or flange. Use a suitable seal removal tool to remove the seal from the housing.

Make sure the housing and yoke or flange are free from nicks and burrs that could impede seal installation or cause seal failure. Install the seal in the housing using a seal installer. Lubricate the lips of the seal with transfer case fluid and install the yoke or flange. Hold the yoke or flange, install the nut and tighten to specification.

Connect the front or rear driveshaft to the output shaft flange or yoke, aligning the marks made prior to removal. Check the fluid level in the transfer case and adjust as required. Lower the vehicle.

Shifter And Linkage

Inspect the shifter mechanism for looseness and binding and make sure that it is mounted securely. Inspect the shift rod and levers for cracks, bending, worn or missing bushings and elongated or distorted holes.

If the shift linkage is adjustable, first loosen the adjuster. Place the shifter and the transfer case shift lever in the same position. Adjust the fit of the shift rod in the levers, and then tighten the adjuster.

Transfer Case Removal

Raise and safely support the vehicle. Remove the skid plate, if equipped. Position a drain pan under the transfer case, remove the drain plug and drain the

Transfer Case Disassembly

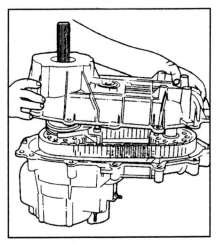

Removing the transfer case cover from the transfer case.
(Courtesy: Ford Motor Co.)

Remove the mounting bolts and the extension housing from the transfer case cover. Remove the snapring from the output shaft that retains the output shaft bearing. Remove the transfer case cover retaining bolts. Insert a prybar or screwdriver between the pry bosses and pry the case and cover apart. Remove the cover from the case.

Use a suitable puller to remove the front output shaft inner needle bearing from the transfer case cover. Use a suitable driver to remove the rear output shaft bearing from the cover, being careful not to damage the bore in the cover.

Transfer case removal. *(Courtesy: Ford Motor Co.)*

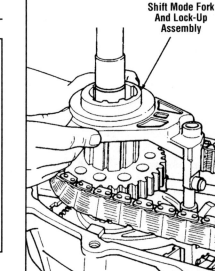

Removing the shift fork and lockup assembly from the output shaft.
(Courtesy: Ford Motor Co.)

fluid from the transfer case.

Label and disconnect the electrical connectors from the transfer case. If equipped with manual shift linkage, disconnect the shift linkage at the shifter or transfer case. Mark the position of the front and rear driveshafts on the output shaft flanges or yokes and remove the driveshafts.

Disconnect the vent hose from the transfer case. Support the transfer case with a transmission jack. Remove the bolts securing the transfer case to the transmission. Slide the transfer case rearward off the transmission output shaft and lower the transfer case from the vehicle.

NOTE: *The following is a general description of the disassembly of a part time chain driven transfer case. Refer to the vehicle service manual for specific overhaul procedures.*

Remove the transfer case from the vehicle. Thoroughly clean the exterior of the transfer case and position it on a bench. Hold the output shaft yokes or flanges with a suitable holding tool and remove the nuts retaining the yokes or flanges to the output shafts, then remove both yokes or flanges. Use a suitable seal removal tool to remove the seals from the housing.

Remove the snapring and 4WD hub from the output shaft. Remove the 2W-4W shift lockup assembly and shift fork assembly from the output shaft. Remove the internal snapring and disassemble the 2W-4W lockup assembly. Remove the snapring from the front output shaft. Remove the drive and driven sprockets with the chain from the transfer case.

Remove the shift rail and high-low shift fork. Remove the output shaft with the pump assembled on it. Remove the high-low shift hub. Remove the input shaft bearing snapring and remove the input shaft and planetary gear assembly. Remove the internal snapring and remove the planetary gear assembly ring gear.

Remove the input and output shaft bearing snaprings and drive the bearings from the case. Remove the shift lever, shift cam, assist spring and bushing from the case.

Component Inspection

Clean all parts in solvent and dry with compressed air. Inspect the transfer case and cover for cracks, worn or damaged bearing bores, worn bushings, stripped threads or other damage, and replace as necessary. Stripped threads can be repaired with suitable thread repair inserts. Inspect all machined surfaces for burrs, nicks and gouges that could inhibit sealing or cause misalignment. Small imperfections can be removed with a file or stone.

Inspect all gears for cracked and damaged teeth. Inspect the shaft surfaces for galling and other wear. Inspect the shaft splines for distortion or other wear or damage. Inspect the drive chain for wear and worn pins and inspect the sprockets for worn teeth.

Disassemble the transfer case pump and inspect for wear, damage and excessive clearance. Inspect all needle and ball bearings for visible wear and roughness when rotated. Inspect the shift forks, shift collar, hubs and springs for wear and damage.

Transfer Case Assembly

Lubricate all parts with transfer case lubricant prior to assembly. Install the input shaft and front output shaft bearings using a suitable driver. Install the front output shaft seal using a seal installer.

Install the front output shaft through the lower bearing. Lubricate the lips of the front out-

put shaft seal and install the front output shaft yoke on the output shaft. Hold the yoke with a suitable tool and torque the retaining nut to specification.

Press a new needle bearing and bushing into the input shaft and planetary gear assembly. Install the ring gear and secure with the internal snapring. Install the input shaft and planetary gear assembly in the case through the input shaft bearing, aligning the gear teeth with the ring gear teeth.

Support the planetary gear assembly and install a new snapring on the front side of the input shaft bearing. Install a new input shaft oil seal using a seal installer.

Install a new shift lever shaft seal in the case. Assemble the shift cam and lever to the case. Assemble the oil pump to the output shaft. Install the high-low shift hub. Engage the shift fork to the shift hub flange and install the shift rail through the high-low fork bore and into the rail bore in the case.

Install the output shaft and oil pump assembly in the input shaft, making sure the output shaft splines engage the high-low shift hub splines. Position the oil pump retainer and oil filter.

Assemble the drive and driven sprockets to the chain and install the chain and sprockets over the rear and front output shafts. Install the snapring retaining the sprocket to the output shaft. Assemble the shift collar, hub and spring of the 2W-4W lockup

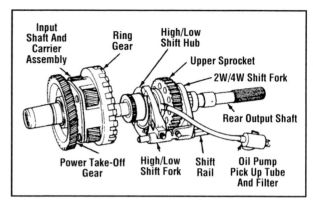

Transfer case internal drivetrain components. *(Courtesy: Ford Motor Co.)*

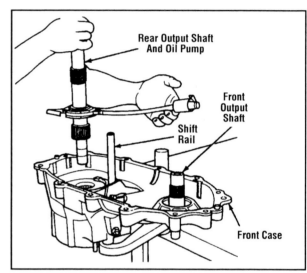

Installing the output shaft and oil pump assembly in the transfer case. *(Courtesy: Ford Motor Co.)*

assembly and secure with the snapring. Install the lockup assembly and shift fork over the drive sprocket and shift rail. Install the return spring over the shift rail and against the shift fork. Place the 4WD hub over the output shaft splines and secure with the snapring.

Press the rear output shaft bearing into the transfer case cover. Install the bearing snapring retainer. Install a new output shaft seal using a seal installer.

Apply a small bead of silicone sealer to the mating surface of the transfer case. Align the front output shaft, shift shaft and shift rail and install the cover to the case. Install the mounting bolts

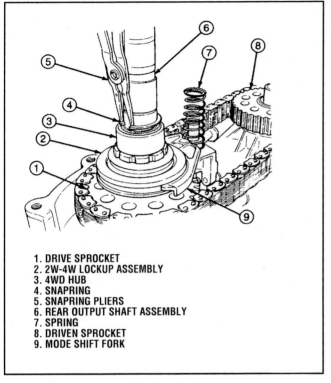

1. DRIVE SPROCKET
2. 2W-4W LOCKUP ASSEMBLY
3. 4WD HUB
4. SNAPRING
5. SNAPRING PLIERS
6. REAR OUTPUT SHAFT ASSEMBLY
7. SPRING
8. DRIVEN SPROCKET
9. MODE SHIFT FORK

Install the lockup assembly and shift fork, then install the 4WD hub and secure with the snapring. (Courtesy: Ford Motor Co.)

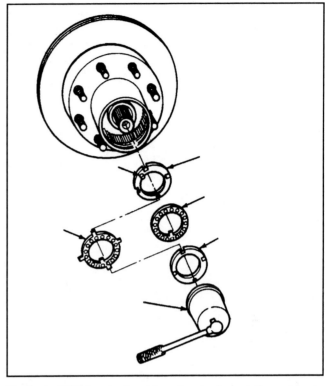

Typical 4WD front wheel bearing lockwasher and locknut arrangement. (Courtesy: Ford Motor Co.)

and torque to specification.

Install the rear bearing snapring onto the output shaft. Apply a small bead of silicone sealer to the mating surface of the extension housing, install the housing and torque the bolts to specification. Using suitable removal and installation tools, remove and install a new extension housing bushing and seal.

Lubricate the lips of the output shaft seal and install the output shaft yoke. Hold the yoke with a suitable holder tool and tighten the output shaft yoke nut to specification.

Transfer Case Installation

Clean the transfer case and transmission gasket surfaces and install a new gasket between the transfer case and adapter. Raise the transfer case into position. Align the transmission output shaft and transfer case input shaft and slide the transfer case forward, aligning the case with the dowel pin. Install the transfer case

retaining bolts and torque to specification.

Connect the driveshafts to the output shaft flanges or yokes, aligning the marks made prior to removal. Connect the vent hose and the electrical connectors. If equipped with a manual shifter, connect the shift control rod.

Install the skid plate, if equipped. Make sure the drain plug is tightened, then fill the transfer case with the proper type of fluid. Install the fill plug and lower the vehicle.

Front Axle Shaft, Bearings And Steering Knuckle

Raise and safely support the vehicle. Remove the wheel. Remove the brake caliper from the rotor and wire it aside. Remove the locking hub retaining bolts, remove the lockring and remove the locking hub assembly from the wheel hub.

Using the special socket required, remove the outer locknut from the spindle. Remove the

lockwasher and using the socket, remove the inner locknut. Remove the hub and rotor assembly from the spindle.

Remove the nuts retaining the spindle to the knuckle. Dislodge the spindle from the knuckle by tapping on it with a plastic mallet. Remove the spindle from the knuckle. Remove the splash shield from the knuckle.

Pull the axle shaft out of the steering knuckle. Disconnect the tie-rod end from the steering knuckle. Remove the kingpin or disconnect the ball joints, as required, and remove the knuckle from the axle shaft.

Remove the outer wheel bearing from the hub. Remove the wheel seal and remove the inner wheel bearing from the hub. Thoroughly clean the wheel bearings and the hub and races with solvent and dry with compressed air. Thoroughly clean the spindle and spindle needle bearing.

Inspect the wheel bearings and races and spindle needle bearing

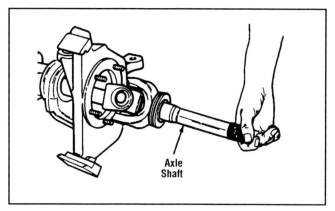

Removing the axle shaft from the axle housing and knuckle. *(Courtesy: Ford Motor Co.)*

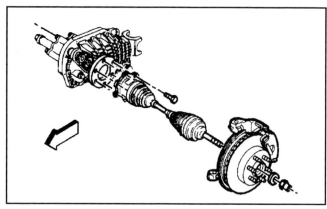

Typical 4WD front halfshaft installation. *(Courtesy: GM Corp.)*

for cracks, pitting, galling, roughness or other damage and replace as necessary. Examine the bearing contact surfaces of the spindle for wear or damage and replace as necessary. If the wheel bearings require replacement, drive the bearing races from the hub. If the needle bearing requires replacement, drive the needle bearing from the spindle.

Pack the wheel bearings and hub with high temperature wheel bearing grease and install the inner bearing in the hub. Install a new wheel seal. Pack a new needle bearing with high temperature grease and install it in the spindle. Install the thrust washer and a new seal in the spindle.

Install the steering knuckle to the axle and install the kingpin or connect the ball joints, as required. Connect the tie-rod end to the steering knuckle. Slide the axle through the knuckle and into the axle housing, aligning the splines of the axle shaft with those on the differential side gear.

Install the splash shield and the spindle. Tighten the spindle nuts to specification. Lubricate the spindle with wheel bearing grease. Install the hub and rotor assembly with the outer wheel bearing. Install the locknuts and lockwasher and adjust the wheel bearings per the manufacturer's instructions. This usually involves tightening the inner locknut to seat the bearings and backing the nut off. The lockwasher is then installed. The outer locknut is then tightened to a specific torque specification.

Install the locking hub body and cap with the cap retaining bolts. Install the caliper and the wheel. Lower the vehicle.

Front Halfshaft

Raise and safely support the vehicle. Remove the wheel and, if equipped, remove the center cap from the hub.

Insert a large drift through the brake caliper into one of the brake rotor vanes to keep the wheel from turning. Remove the nut and washer from the halfshaft stub shaft and discard the nut. Remove the mounting bolts securing the inboard CV-joint housing to the differential output shaft flange.

Use a suitable tool to press the stub shaft from the hub. Remove the drift and remove the halfshaft from the vehicle. Components like sway bar links may have to be disconnected and removed to provide access for the halfshaft. Take care to protect the CV-joint boots as the halfshaft is removed.

Carefully position the halfshaft in the vehicle. Insert the stub shaft through the wheel hub and install the washer with a new nut. Do not tighten at this time.

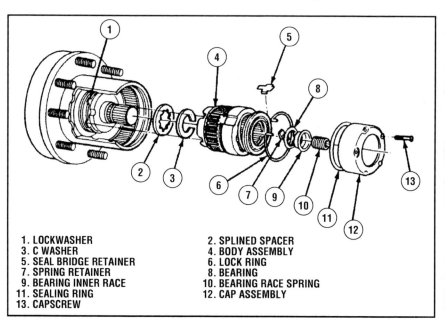

1. LOCKWASHER
2. SPLINED SPACER
3. C WASHER
4. BODY ASSEMBLY
5. SEAL BRIDGE RETAINER
6. LOCK RING
7. SPRING RETAINER
8. BEARING
9. BEARING INNER RACE
10. BEARING RACE SPRING
11. SEALING RING
12. CAP ASSEMBLY
13. CAPSCREW

Exploded view of a typical automatic locking hub assembly. *(Courtesy: Ford Motor Co.)*

Secure the inboard CV-joint housing to the differential output shaft flange with the mounting bolts. Reinstall the drift and torque the inboard flange mounting bolts and the stub shaft nut to specification. Remove the drift.

Install any components that were removed to provide halfshaft access. Install the hub center cap and wheel. Lower the vehicle.

Locking Hubs

Locking hubs usually fail or are difficult to engage or disengage because the seal has failed and allowed dirt and moisture to enter the unit.

Remove the locking hub cap retaining bolts and remove the cap. Be prepared to catch any springs or bearings as the cap is removed. Remove the lockring from the hub and remove the locking hub assembly.

Disassemble and clean the hub components. Inspect all components for wear and corrosion. Replace parts or the entire locking hub assembly, as required.

Lubricate components with the required lubricant during assembly. Adjust the wheel bearings before the locking hub is installed. Install the locking hub cap with a new rubber seal and torque the cap retaining bolts to manufacturer's specification.

Vacuum Motor Actuators

Vacuum motors may fail to lock or unlock the front axle if the motor does not operate due to a vacuum leak or failed diaphragm, or due to internal linkage that is worn or stuck. Check the vacuum motor diaphragm with a vacuum pump. If the diaphragm is not leaking, check for vacuum leaks and a bad vacuum switch.

If the transfer case is definitely in 4WD, the diaphragm and vacuum switch are good, there are no vacuum leaks and the axle does not lock or unlock properly, remove the mounting bolts and remove the vacuum motor assembly from the axle housing. Connect the vacuum lines to the vacuum motor, shift in and out of 4WD

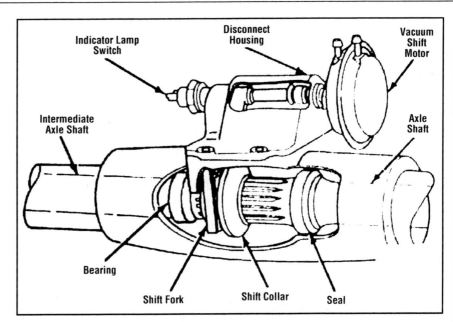

Cutaway view of a vacuum shift motor assembly.
(Courtesy: DaimlerChrysler Corp.)

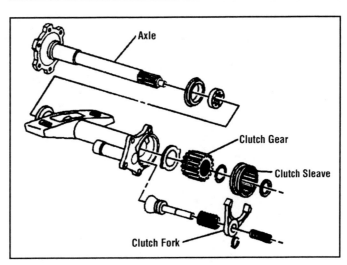

Typical part time 4WD front axle actuating assembly.
(Courtesy: GM Corp.)

and check the movement of the vacuum motor shaft. If the shaft does not move as far as it should, the vacuum motor is defective and should be replaced. If the shaft moves properly, check for binding at the shift fork and collar.

Electric Motor Actuators

The front axle on a vehicle with an electric motor actuator may fail to connect or disconnect in response to the 4WD switch because of a problem with the electrical circuit or control system, a failed actuator motor or a stuck or broken actuating assembly.

Some transfer cases are controlled by the PCM (Powertrain Control Module) or a TCM (Transmission Control Module) and have self-diagnostic capabilities. Consult the vehicle service manual for the proper diagnostic procedure. If the axle does not lock when 4WD is selected, make sure that the motor is receiving power when 4WD is commanded. If there is power to the motor, try removing it from the axle to see if the plunger that acts on the clutch fork extends when 4WD is selected. If the motor is working, then the problem is in the axle actuating assembly.

NOTES

Prepare yourself for ASE testing with these questions on
MANUAL DRIVETRAIN AND AXLES

NOTE: The following questions are written in the ASE style. They are similar to the kinds of questions that you will see on the ASE test, however none of these questions will actually appear on the test.

1. A clutch disc is removed and found to be oil soaked. Technician A says it can be cleaned using solvent. Technician B says it can be sanded and reused. Who is right?

    A. Technician A only
    B. Technician B only
    C. Both A and B
    D. Neither A or B

2. Technician A says that engine/transmission misalignment can cause a pulsation in the clutch pedal. Technician B says that if there is excessive runout at the face of the bell housing, and the surface is not parallel with the rear of the engine block, it can be corrected using offset dowel pins. Who is right?

    A. Technician A only
    B. Technician B only
    C. Both A and B
    D. Neither A or B

3. Clutch slippage can be caused by all of the following **EXCEPT**:

    A. worn clutch disc
    B. excessive free-play
    C. oil contaminated friction surfaces
    D. weak pressure plate springs

4. A customer that has never owned a 4WD vehicle before just purchased an SUV with part time 4WD. After driving the vehicle a short time, he complains that the vehicle steers wide (understeers) in turns. Which of the following should be your response?

    A. Tell him there is probably something wrong with the steering.
    B. Tell him that all 4WD vehicles handle that way.
    C. Tell him that he's just not used to a new vehicle and needs to drive it more to be more comfortable with its handling.
    D. Ask him if he's driving in 4WD all the time.

5. When setting up a ring and pinion, checking the gear tooth contact pattern is used to check what setting?

    A. differential bearing preload
    B. pinion bearing preload
    C. pinion depth
    D. differential case runout

6. A rear-wheel drive vehicle with a one-piece driveshaft has excessive driveshaft vibration during low speed acceleration. Which of the following is the **MOST** likely cause?

    A. binding U-joints
    B. excessive driveshaft runout
    C. driveshaft out of balance
    D. improper driveshaft angle

7. When discussing a synchronizer assembly, all of the following statements are true **EXCEPT**:

    A. The position of the hub in the sleeve should be marked prior to disassembly.
    B. The sleeve should be a tight fit on the hub.
    C. The synchronizer blocking ring teeth should be pointed but smooth and not rounded off.
    D. The grooves on the inside of the blocking ring should be clearly defined.

8. Technician A says that if a transmission is hard to shift into gear, the problem is most likely with the clutch. Technician B says that hard shifting can be caused by binding shift linkage or synchronizers. Who is right?

    A. Technician A only
    B. Technician B only
    C. Both A and B
    D. Neither A or B

9. Technician A says that the chain and sprockets in a transfer case are removed and installed on the shafts as an assembly. Technician B says the drive chain should be inspected for wear and worn pins and the sprockets inspected for worn teeth. Who is right?

    A. Technician A only
    B. Technician B only
    C. Both A and B
    D. Neither A or B

Prepare yourself for ASE testing with these questions on
MANUAL DRIVETRAIN AND AXLES

10. Technician A says that timing marks must be aligned when a hunting type gear set is installed. Technician B says that a non-hunting gear set can be installed in any mesh position. Who is right?
   - A. Technician A only
   - B. Technician B only
   - C. Both A and B
   - D. Neither A or B

11. Technician A says the 1st-2nd synchronizer assembly speeds up the countershaft when shifting from first to second. Technician B says the 1st-2nd synchronizer assembly speeds up the main shaft when shifting from first to second. Who is right?
   - A. Technician A only
   - B. Technician B only
   - C. Both A and B
   - E. Neither A or B

12. A clicking noise is heard on a front-wheel drive vehicle while turning a corner. Technician A says that a worn outboard CV-joint could be the cause. Technician B says that the noise could be coming from a worn inboard CV-joint. Who is right?
   - A. Technician A only
   - B. Technician B only
   - C. Both A and B
   - D. Neither A or B

13. A rear-wheel drive vehicle with a one-piece driveshaft has excessive runout at the rear of the driveshaft. After repositioning the driveshaft on the pinion flange 180 degrees from its original position, there is still excessive runout, but the runout high points are on opposite sides of the driveshaft. Technician A says that the driveshaft is bent and must be replaced. Technician B says that the differential pinion flange could be the problem. Who is right?
   - A. Technician A only
   - B. Technician B only
   - C. Both A and B
   - D. Neither A or B

14. Two technicians are installing a transmission in a rear wheel-drive vehicle, however, the transmission case will not seat against the bell housing. Technician A says that, since it is so close, the transmission can be drawn into place using the transmission mounting

bolts. Technician B says that the transmission should be removed and clutch disc alignment should be rechecked. Who is right?
   - A. Technician A only
   - B. Technician B only
   - C. Both A and B
   - D. Neither A or B

15. A front-wheel drive vehicle with a manual transaxle has excessive vibration. Technician A says that the vibration could be caused by worn engine/transaxle mounts. Technician B says that the vibration could be caused by a misaligned engine/transaxle subframe. Who is right?
   - A. Technician A only
   - B. Technician B only
   - C. Both A and B
   - D. Neither A or B

16. A customer complains of having a more difficult time getting traction on slippery roads than in past winters and asks whether his limited slip differential is functioning. Technician A says that the differential must be disassembled to make a determination. Technician B says that the differential does not require disassembly to be tested. Who is right?
   - A. Technician A only
   - B. Technician B only
   - C. Both A and B
   - D. Neither A or B

17. Excessive clutch pedal free-play can cause:
   - A. premature release bearing wear
   - B. the engine to race when the vehicle is accelerated
   - C. a grinding noise when shifting into gear
   - D. a noisy release bearing

18. A 4WD truck with a vacuum shift motor on the front axle will not go into four-wheel drive. The transfer case goes into four-wheel drive, there are no vacuum leaks, and the vacuum motor diaphragm is OK when tested with a vacuum pump. Technician A says that the problem must be binding at the shift fork and collar inside the axle. Technician B says that the vacuum motor could still be defective. Who is right?
   - A. Technician A only
   - B. Technician B only
   - C. Both A and B
   - D. Neither A or B

19. A two-piece driveshaft is being installed in a light truck. Technician A says that the splined coupling shaft can be installed in the slip yoke in any position. Technician B says that the splines should be lubricated prior to installation. Who is right?

    A. Technician A only
    B. Technician B only
    C. Both A and B
    D. Neither A or B

20. When inspecting the transmission main (output) shaft, all of the following should be done **EXCEPT**:

    A. measure the shaft runout using a dial indicator
    B. check the splines for rust, burrs or other wear
    C. check the gear teeth for wear, pits, cracks and chipped teeth
    D. measure the diameter and check all main shaft journals for wear or damage

21. Evidence of oil contamination has been found on the clutch assembly of a rear-wheel drive vehicle after bell housing removal. The oil could be coming from any of the following **EXCEPT**:

    A. leaking cam plug
    B. worn rear main seal
    C. worn transmission extension housing seal
    D. worn transmission input shaft bearing retainer seal

22. Technician A says that transaxle differential side and pinion gears should be replaced if they are scuffed or have broken teeth. Technician B says that when the differential is assembled, side gear end-play should be checked with a feeler gauge and shimmed accordingly. Who is right?

    A. Technician A only
    B. Technician B only
    C. Both A and B
    D. Neither A or B

23. Technician A says that improper driveline angle can be corrected by placing shims between the transmission mount and crossmember. Technician B says that installing shims between the rear springs and rear axle spring seats can correct a driveline angle that is not within specifications. Who is right?

    A. Technician A only
    B. Technician B only
    C. Both A and B
    D. Neither A or B

24. Before removing a flywheel from the crankshaft flange, a technician attaches a dial indicator base to the engine block and positions the dial indicator so the foot rests on the surface of the flywheel. All of the following can be determined with this setup **EXCEPT**:

    A. flywheel thickness
    B. flywheel runout
    C. crankshaft end-play
    D. crankshaft thrust bearing clearance

25. Excessive clearance between the input shaft and main shaft can cause the transmission to jump out of what gear?

    A. first gear
    B. second gear
    C. third gear
    D. fourth gear

26. Gold particles and silver flakes are found in oil that has been drained from a manual transaxle. Technician A says that the gold particles are from worn synchronizer blocking rings. Technician B says that the silver flakes are from worn gears. Who is right?

    A. Technician A only
    B. Technician B only
    C. Both A and B
    D. Neither A or B

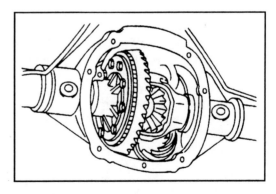

27. There is not enough ring gear backlash on the rear axle assembly shown above, but the bearing preload is correct. Which of the following should the technician do to increase backlash?

    A. add shim thickness to the left side and decrease the same thickness on the left
    B. add shim thickness to the right side and decrease the same thickness on the left
    C. add the same amount of shim thickness to both sides
    D. decrease the shim thickness on both sides

Prepare yourself for ASE testing with these questions on
MANUAL DRIVETRAIN AND AXLES

28. A transmission synchronizer blocking ring is being inspected. Technician A says that the blocking ring can be reused as long as the teeth are pointed but smooth and not rounded off, the grooves on the inside of the blocking ring where it contacts the gear cone are clearly defined all the way around, and the insert notches are square. Technician B says that the blocking ring to gear clearance must be measured. Who is right?
    A. Technician A only
    B. Technician B only
    C. Both A and B
    D. Neither A or B

29. When the clutch pedal is depressed on a vehicle with hydraulic clutch linkage, the clutch does not disengage. Which of the following could be the cause?
    A. worn pressure plate springs
    B. insufficient clutch pedal free-play
    C. worn clutch disc
    D. air in the hydraulic system

30. When discussing transmission shift linkage, all of the following are true statements **EXCEPT**:
    A. only external shift linkage is adjustable
    B. adjustment is usually done with the transmission in neutral
    C. linkage rods that are cracked, bent or have elongated bushing holes should be replaced
    D. the linkage must be replaced as an assembly

31. During the overhaul of a differential, the following components were cleaned, inspected and appeared to be in reusable condition. However, which component should still not be reused, regardless of how it appears?
    A. rear pinion bearing
    B. differential bearing preload shim
    C. differential pinion shaft
    D. collapsible spacer

32. A new clutch disc and pressure plate is being installed on a rear-wheel drive vehicle. Technician A says that the clutch disc should be installed with the torsion spring offset section facing the flywheel. Technician B says that the pressure plate bolts should be tightened gradually in a criss-cross pattern until the pressure plate is drawn against the flywheel, and then torqued to specification. Who is right?
    A. Technician A only
    B. Technician B only
    C. Both A and B
    D. Neither A or B

33. The transmission countergear usually rotates on:
    A. bushings
    B. roller bearings
    C. tapered roller bearings
    D. sealed bearings

34. A halfshaft is being removed from a front-wheel drive vehicle. If the outboard stub shaft will not come free from the wheel hub, Technician A says the stub shaft can be driven out using a hammer and a brass drift. After the stub shaft is free of the hub, Technician B says that the halfshaft can be removed from the differential side gear by pulling on the interconnecting shaft. Who is right?
    A. Technician A only
    B. Technician B only
    C. Both A and B
    D. Neither A or B

35. A front-wheel drive vehicle with a manual transaxle exhibits a clunking sound during acceleration and deceleration. All of the following could be the cause **EXCEPT**:
    A. excessive countergear end-play
    B. worn inboard CV-joint
    C. loose engine/transaxle mounts
    D. worn differential pinion shaft

36. With the clutch pedal fully depressed and the transmission in gear, a noise is heard coming from the bell housing area. Technician A says that the noise could be caused by a worn pilot bushing. Technician B says that the noise is probably due to a defective transmission input shaft bearing. Who is right?
    A. Technician A only
    B. Technician B only
    C. Both A and B
    D. Neither A or B

37. The front axle on a 4WD truck was completely rebuilt with all new bearings and seals, however, after a short period of time it has begun to leak gear oil again. Which of the following is the **MOST** likely cause?
    A. defective seals
    B. incorrect installation
    C. improper grade lubricant
    D. clogged axle vent

38. When replacing the transmission extension housing bushing and seal, which of the following should also be inspected?
  A. output shaft bearing
  B. extension housing gasket
  C. driveshaft slip yoke
  D. speedometer drive O-ring

39. Before a differential case is removed, the ring gear runout is measured using a dial indicator and found to be excessive. Which of the following is the **MOST** correct course of action for the technician?
  A. replace the ring gear, it is defective
  B. decrease differential bearing preload to correct the runout
  C. increase backlash to allow for the runout
  D. measure differential case runout with the ring gear removed

40. A pinion seal is being replaced on a rear-wheel drive vehicle with drum brakes. Technician A says that only the driveshaft and pinion flange need be removed. Technician B says that the wheels and brake drums must also be removed. Who is right?
  A. Technician A only
  B. Technician B only
  C. Both A and B
  D. Neither A or B

41. All of the following defective rear axle components would make more noise when the vehicle is turning a corner **EXCEPT**:
  A. limited slip differential clutch packs
  B. differential case bearings
  C. axle shaft bearings
  D. differential side gears

42. The transfer case on a 4WD truck with manual shift linkage will not shift into 4WD. Which of the following could be the cause?
  A. rusted locking hubs
  B. low transfer case fluid level
  C. misadjusted shift linkage
  D. a vacuum leak

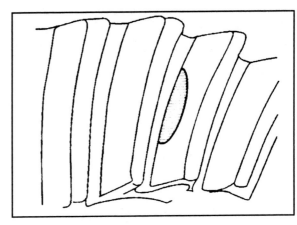

43. After setting up a new ring and pinion, a technician checks the gear tooth contact pattern and sees the pattern shown above. Which of the following should he do?
  A. Move the pinion gear closer to the ring gear.
  B. Move the pinion gear away from the ring gear.
  C. Move the ring gear closer to the pinion gear.
  D. Move the ring gear away from the pinion gear.

44. Technician A says that, when the locking hubs of a vehicle with part time 4WD are disengaged and the transfer case is in 2H, the entire front drivetrain does not turn. Technician B says that, when the vacuum shift motor and front axle disconnect mechanism of a vehicle with part time 4WD is disengaged and the transfer case is in 2H, the axles and differential gears turn, but the ring and pinion and driveshaft do not. Who is right?
  A. Technician A only
  B. Technician B only
  C. Both A and B
  D. Neither A or B

45. A growling noise is heard coming from a rear axle. Which of the following could be the cause?
  A. improper gear tooth contact pattern
  B. faulty bearings
  C. excessive ring gear runout
  D. excessive differential case runout

46. A vehicle with hydraulic clutch linkage has a hard pedal. Any of the following could be the cause **EXCEPT**:
  A. contaminated hydraulic fluid
  B. restricted hydraulic line
  C. low fluid level
  D. blocked master cylinder compensating port

47. A start/clutch interlock switch is being tested. Technician A says that, with the clutch pedal in the released position, the switch should have continuity when checked with an ohmmeter. Technician B says that, with the pedal depressed, there should be voltage on both sides of the switch when checked with a voltmeter. Who is right?

    A. Technician A only
    B. Technician B only
    C. Both A and B
    D. Neither A or B

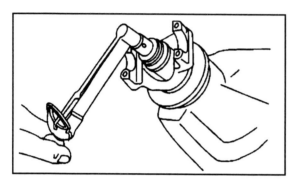

48. In the procedure shown above, Technician A says the reading should be taken while the pinion nut is being turned. Technician B says the reading should be taken when the pinion nut begins to turn. Who is right?

    A. Technician A only
    B. Technician B only
    C. Both A and B
    D. Neither A or B

49. Which of the following is the **MOST** common cause of clutch chatter?

    A. worn input shaft splines
    B. weak clutch disc torsional springs
    C. scored flywheel
    D. fluid contamination

50. When replacing an integral hub/bearing assembly on a front-wheel drive vehicle, all of the following must be removed **EXCEPT**:

    A. brake rotor
    B. brake caliper
    C. steering knuckle
    D. wheel

NOTES

Answers to Study-Guide Test Questions

1. The correct answer is D. It is impossible to remove oil that has become impregnated in the clutch disc friction lining. Regardless of how clean the surface looks, oil will eventually rise to the surface and affect clutch operation. Also, solvents can contain traces of oil themselves and should not be used to clean the clutch disc. When a clutch disc is inspected, unless it is undamaged and has very little wear, it should be replaced.

2. The correct answer is A. Engine/transmission misalignment can cause noise when the clutch is engaged and can cause pulsation in the clutch pedal. Technician B is incorrect because offset dowel pins are used to correct excessive bell housing bore runout. Placing shim stock between the bell housing and block is the way to correct excessive bell housing face runout.

3. The correct answer is B. Excessive free-play would not cause the clutch to slip, however, insufficient free-play would, since insufficient free-play causes the release bearing to apply pressure to the pressure plate while in the released position. The other three answers can all be causes of clutch slippage. As the friction lining becomes thinner on a worn clutch disc, the pressure plate will not be able to exert as much spring pressure and clamping force on the disc, causing clutch slippage. Weak pressure plate springs would also not have enough clamping power on the friction disc. A lubricant on the friction surfaces would cause slippage.

4. The correct answer is D. As its name suggests, part time 4WD is not meant to be used all the time. Unfortunately, many drivers are not aware of this, with unfortunate consequences. When any vehicle turns, the front wheels track differently and with different wheel speed than those on the rear. However, the transfer case on a part time 4WD vehicle turns both driveshafts at the same speed when in 4WD, which does not allow the front wheels to turn at a different speed than the rears. When a part time 4WD vehicle is driven in 4WD on dirt or ice and snow, this is not a problem, because the wheels can slip. But when used on dry pavement, hard steering, like that experienced by the customer, will be the result. If 4WD continues to be used on dry pavement, the vehicle will experience 'driveline windup', where the mechanical parts in the driveline begin to bind and then break.

5. The correct answer is C. Pinion depth is the distance from the face of the pinion gear to the centerline of the ring gear. The initial pinion depth measurement and shim selection procedure are only to estab-lish a base setting. The final pinion depth is determined by checking the gear tooth contact pattern.

6. The correct answer is D. All of the choices can cause driveshaft vibration, however, vibration during heavy acceleration or deceleration, especially at lower speeds, is probably due to incorrect driveshaft angle. The most common cause of driveshaft angle problems is incorrect vehicle ride height.

7. The correct answer is B. The synchronizer sleeve must slide freely on the hub or hard shifting could result. All of the other statements are true concerning synchronizer assemblies.

8. The correct answer is C, both technicians. If the transmission is hard to shift into gear, the problem is usually with the clutch not releasing completely. However, hard shifting can also be due to shift linkage that is binding or improperly adjusted, or binding gears and/or synchronizers.

9. The correct answer is C, both technicians. A worn transfer case drive chain can cause noise and should be inspected as described when the transfer case is apart. The drive and driven sprockets are removed and installed with the chain as an assembly.

10. The correct answer is D, neither technician. Hunting gear sets, where any one pinion gear tooth contacts all ring gear teeth, are not marked and can be installed in any mesh position. On non-hunting type gear sets, where any one pinion gear tooth contacts only a certain number of teeth, the marks on the ring and pinion gear must be aligned when they are installed.

11. The correct answer is D, neither technician. The synchronizer brings the gear to the same speed as the main shaft, then locks the gear to the synchronizer hub and the main shaft so power can be delivered through that gear.

12. The correct answer is A. If a clicking or snapping noise is heard when accelerating around a corner, suspect a worn outboard CV-joint. Outboard CV-joints usually wear more quickly than inboard joints because the outboard joint operates at much more extreme angles than inboard joints. Turning does not affect an inboard CV-joint.

13. The correct answer is B. When driveshaft

runout is checked, the high point should be marked. When runout is rechecked after the driveshaft is repositioned 180 degrees, again mark the high point. If the two high point marks are within about an inch of one another, the driveshaft is bent and must be replaced. However, if the marks are about 180 degrees apart, then the pinion flange is responsible. In the question, the high point marks were on opposite sides of the driveshaft, 180 degrees apart, so technician B is correct.

14. The correct answer is B. Technician A is wrong because the transmission should never be forced into place. Damage to the pilot bearing, transmission input shaft or other components could result. If the transmission will not install properly, remove it and determine the problem. Check clutch disc alignment using an old input shaft or clutch alignment tool.

15. The correct answer is C, both technicians. Worn engine and transaxle mounts can cause vibration, but driveline vibration can also be caused by an engine/transaxle subframe that is damaged or not properly positioned and secured to the vehicle.

16. The correct answer is B. The operation of a limited slip differential can be checked by measuring the torque required to turn one wheel while the other is held. One of the rear wheels is raised off the ground and a suitable adapter is attached that goes over the lug nuts and provides for torque wrench attachment. Place the transmission in neutral, turn the wheel with a torque wrench and note the reading when the wheel begins to turn. The reading when the wheel begins to turn is the break-away torque, and may be higher than the continuous turning torque. Compare the break-away torque reading to specification. If the torque reading is lower than specification, the clutch packs or preload springs in the limited slip differential are probably worn.

17. The correct answer is C. If the transmission makes a grinding noise when going into gear, the clutch is dragging and not releasing properly. Excessive free-play is the most common cause for a dragging clutch. All of the other choices would be caused by insufficient clutch pedal free-play.

18. The correct answer is B. Remove the vacuum motor assembly from the axle housing and connect the vacuum lines to the vacuum motor, shift in and out of 4WD and check the movement of the vacuum motor shaft. Compare the actual movement with specifications. If the shaft does not move as far as it should, the vacuum motor is defective and should be replaced. Although the possible cause described by technician A was valid, it was not the only remaining possibility.

19. The correct answer is B. The splines on the coupling shaft and slip yoke should be lubricated with grease prior to installation. Most slip yokes with multi-piece driveshafts are also equipped with grease fittings and must be lubricated periodically. Technician A is wrong because the coupling shaft must engage with the slip yoke so the U-joint yokes are on the same plane, 'in phase', or the assembly will be imbalanced resulting in vibration.

20. The correct answer is C. The gears are not integral components of the main shaft, but rather turn on the main shaft and are locked in position by the synchronizer assemblies when the transmission is shifted. Therefore, gear teeth inspection is not a part of main shaft inspection.

21. The correct answer is C. The transmission extension housing seal could not be the cause of the oil contamination because it is at the other end of the transmission. Any of the other choices could be the source of oil inside the bell housing.

22. The correct answer is A. Differential side and pinion gears should be replaced if these defects are found. Technician B is wrong because side gear end-play is checked with a dial indicator and corrected with different thickness thrust washers.

23. The correct answer is C, both technicians. Installing shims between the transmission mount and crossmember can restore the proper engine/transmission angle. Placing shims between the rear springs and rear axle springs seats or between the rear axle and control arms can correct the driveshaft/pinion angle.

24. The correct answer is A. Flywheel thickness cannot be determined this way. Flywheel runout can be checked using a dial indicator, but you must push in on the flywheel as it is turned to take up the crankshaft thrust bearing clearance. Crankshaft end-play and thrust bearing clearance is the same thing. It is checked by pushing the flywheel forward against the thrust bearing, zeroing the dial indicator, and then prying evenly on both sides of the flywheel to pull it back. If the flywheel has excessive runout, it should be resurfaced or replaced. If the crankshaft thrust bearing clearance is excessive, the thrust bearing and possibly the crankshaft will require replacement.

Answers to Study-Guide Test Questions

25. The correct answer is D. Since fourth gear is usually part of the input shaft, this is the only possible answer. All of the other gears are located farther back on the main shaft and would be unaffected by clearance between the main and input shafts.

26. The correct answer is C, both technicians. The synchronizer blocking rings are made of brass which is gold colored. As the transmission gears wear against one another, silver flakes and particles are produced and appear in the transaxle fluid.

27. The correct answer is B. To increase backlash, the ring gear should be moved toward the left side of the vehicle, away from the pinion, but at the same time the bearing preload must be maintained, therefore, answer B is correct. A is incorrect because this would have the opposite effect and further decrease backlash. C is incorrect because this would increase bearing preload but would not affect backlash. D is incorrect because doing this would decrease bearing preload and at the same time not improve the backlash setting.

28. The correct answer is B. The synchronizer blocking ring must pass all of the requirements listed by Technician A, however, he is wrong because passing a visual inspection is not the only criteria for putting the blocking ring back into service. Technician B is correct because the blocking ring to gear clearance must also be checked. If this clearance is not within specification, the blocking ring must be replaced.

29. The correct answer is D. If there are air bubbles in the hydraulic fluid, the clutch pedal travel could be all used up compressing the air in the system instead of moving the slave cylinder piston and pushrod, resulting in the clutch staying engaged. Answer B is wrong because insufficient clutch pedal free-play would allow the clutch to disengage but could also cause it not to fully engage. Worn pressure plate springs or a worn clutch disc could cause the clutch to slip but would not prevent clutch disengagement.

30. The correct answer is D. Linkage rods and levers can be replaced separately. All of the other choices are true statements concerning transmission shift linkage.

31. The correct answer is D. The collapsible spacer must never be reused, regardless of its appearance.

32. The correct answer is B. Most new clutch discs are marked indicating flywheel side, however, if no mark is present, install the clutch disc with the torsion spring offset section facing away from the flywheel.

33. The correct answer is B. A common design has the countergear supported in the transmission case by a countershaft and several sets of roller bearings.

34. The correct answer is D, neither technician. Technician A is wrong because, if the stub shaft will not pull free from the wheel hub, do not hammer on the stub shaft, but use a suitable puller to remove the shaft from the hub. Technician B is wrong because, pulling on the axle shaft in an effort to separate the stub shaft from the differential side gear can pull apart the inboard CV-joint. A prybar or slide hammer/puller tool should be used to release the inboard stub shaft from the differential side gear.

35. The correct answer is A. A countergear is used in a manual transmission, but not in a manual transaxle. All of the other choices could cause a clunking noise during acceleration and deceleration.

36. The correct answer is A. When the clutch is disengaged and the transmission is in gear, the crankshaft spins around the stationary transmission input shaft. Since, in this instance, the pilot bushing is turning while the input shaft bearing is motionless, of the two choices the pilot bushing can be the only answer.

37. The correct answer is D. The axle can leak if excessive pressure builds up due to a clogged axle vent. It is common for axle vents to become clogged on vehicles that are used off-road, and the axle vent can be forgotten when an axle is overhauled.

38. The correct answer is C. Since the driveshaft slip yoke rides on the extension housing bushing and seal, it should also be checked for wear and damage when the bushing and seal are replaced.

39. The correct answer is D. Excessive runout on the differential case flange could be the cause of the excessive ring gear runout, so the case should be checked before condemning the ring gear. The ring gear and pinion must always be replaced as an assembly as they are a matched set. Answer B is wrong because decreasing differential bearing preload will not correct excessive runout. Answer C is wrong because there is no allowance for runout above that specified by the manufacturer.

40. The correct answer is B. The pinion bearing preload must be checked with an inch pound torque wrench before the pinion flange is removed, and the wheels and brake drums must be removed to prevent drag and a false pinion bearing torque reading.

41. The correct answer is B. Worn differential case bearings will become noisier at increased road speeds but will not be more prevalent when the vehicle is turning a corner. Sticking clutch packs in a limited slip differential can make a chattering sound when cornering and damaged side gears and/or pinion gears can make a clunking sound. Axle shaft bearing noise will increase when the bearing is loaded and can be verified by steering left and right while driving, rocking the vehicle to move the weight more right and left. Bearing noise that is noticeably worse in one direction indicates that the opposite axle shaft bearing is at fault.

42. The correct answer is C. A low transfer case fluid level could cause internal transfer case damage, but they would not prevent the unit from being shifted into 4WD. Seized locking hubs or, if the front axle is engaged with a vacuum shift motor, a vacuum leak, may not allow power to be transferred to the front wheels, but would not prevent the transfer case from shifting into 4WD. However, manual shift linkage that is binding or not adjusted properly, would not allow the transfer case to be shifted.

43. The correct answer is B. In the pattern shown, contact is located toward the root of the tooth, with the length of the pattern longer at the root than at the top. The pinion is too deep and must be shimmed away from the ring gear.

44. The correct answer is C, both technicians. When in 2WD, the front drivetrain on a part time 4WD vehicle with locking hubs does not turn. However, when in 2WD, the front axles and differential gears turn on a vehicle with vacuum shift motor and front axle disconnect mechanism. These vehicles have a two-piece axle, usually located on the passenger side. The outer axle is connected to the wheel and then inner axle to the differential. In 2WD, the driver's side axle rotates, turning the differential side gear. The differential side gear spins the spider gears and in turn spins the opposite differential side gear and the passenger side inner axle backwards. When 4WD is selected, the vacuum shift motor slides a splined shift collar over the ends of the two-piece axle, locking them together.

45. The correct answer is B. Whining or howling noises are usually gear related. A growling sound may be caused by differential, pinion or axle bearings.

46. The correct answer is C. Low fluid level in the master cylinder would cause a soft pedal. All of the other answers could cause a hard pedal, including contaminated fluid, which could make the seals swell and bind in the master cylinder and slave cylinder.

47. The correct answer is B. The start/clutch interlock switch is open when the clutch pedal is in the released position, interrupting current flow in the starter circuit. When the clutch pedal is depressed, the switch closes, allowing current flow in the circuit. Technician A is wrong because an open switch should have no continuity.

48. The correct answer is A. The torque required to initially move the pinion will be higher than that required to keep it in motion. Technician B is wrong because the torque value that is usually needed (for pinion seal replacement, etc.) is that which is required to maintain rotation of the pinion through several revolutions. Using an initial reading would cause bearing preload to be set too high during installation.

49. The correct answer is D. Although all of the answers listed can cause clutch chatter, the most common cause is fluid contamination. Fluid contamination can be from oil, caused by a leaking engine rear main seal or transmission input shaft seal, or from hydraulic fluid from a leaking clutch slave cylinder or hydraulic line.

50. The correct answer is C. The steering knuckle does not have to be removed when replacing an integral hub/bearing assembly. However, it must be removed when replacing the press-fit type front wheel bearing.

Answers to Study-Guide Test Questions

NOTES

Glossary of Terms

-- a --

abrasion - rubbing away or wearing of a part.

all-wheel drive (AWD) - the method of providing traction to any of the wheels of a vehicle, as conditions require. Depending on the system, it may be full-time or part-time.

alloy - the mixture of two or more metals or of a metal and another substance (e.g., solder, an alloy consisting of lead and tin).

aluminum - a light weight metal used often for cylinder heads and other parts.

automatic locking hubs - front-wheel drive hubs that can engage and disengage themselves from the axles automatically.

AWD - see **all-wheel drive.**

axial - around, on or along an axis; having the same direction or being parallel to the axis of rotation.

axial load - a type of load placed on a bearing that is parallel to the axis of the rotating shaft.

axial play - movement of a component parallel to the axis of rotation.

axis - a real or imaginary straight line on which or around which an object rotates.

axle - a rotating shaft that rotates another part, such as a wheel.

axle housing - an enclosure for the differential and drive axles.

--b--

backlash - the clearance or play between moving parts, as in gear mesh.

ball bearing - a friction-reducing bearing that uses a series of steel balls held between inner and outer bearing races such as in a roller clutch.

bearing - part that supports and reduces friction between a stationary and moving part or two moving parts.

bearing clearance - the space between a bearing and its corresponding component's loaded surface. Bearing clearances are commonly provided to allow lubrication between the parts.

bearing race - the machined surface of a bearing assembly against which the needles, balls or rollers ride. The outer race is also called a cup.

bell housing - connects the engine to the transmission and encloses the clutch assembly. It also provides mounting points for part of the clutch release mechanism.

blocking ring - in a manual transmission, part of the synchronizer assembly. A brass ring that brings the driven gear to shaft speed before engagement.

bolt diameter - measurement across the major diameter of a bolt's threaded area or the bolt shank.

bolt head - part of the bolt that the socket or wrench fits over in order to torque or tighten the bolt.

boot - protective rubber cover with accordion pleats used to contain lubricants and exclude contaminating dirt, water and grime, located at each end of the rack-and-pinion assembly and FWD CV-joints.

bore - a cylindrical hole.

break-in - a slow wearing-in process between two mating part surfaces.

burr - a ragged metal edge left on a part during machining.

bushing - a liner, usually removable, for a bearing; an anti-friction liner used in place of a bearing; a type of bearing that is used to support rotating shafts.

--c--

C-clip - part used to retain the axle shaft in a drive axle assembly.

cardan universal joint - the most common type of universal joint used. Consists of a center cross, four bearing cups, each containing a set of needle roller bearings, grease seals and snaprings.

casting - metal that is manufactured by pouring it into a mold. It is more porous than forged metal and does not conduct heat as well. It is less expensive to manufacture, however.

center support bearing - a ball bearing housed in a rubber insulator. Mounted to the underside of a vehicle and used to support the driveshaft when more than one driveshaft is used.

clearance - the specified distance between two components.

Glossary of Terms

clutch - in a manual transmission, a device that allows the driver to engage and disengage the engine from the drivetrain; in an automatic transmission, a device capable of both holding and turning members of a planetary gearset; a device used to engage and disengage an A/C compressor.

clutch disc - the part of a clutch that receives the driving motion from the flywheel and pressure plate assembly and transmits that motion to the transmission input shaft.

clutch facing - the friction material on a clutch disc.

clutch fork - also known as the release fork. The device that moves the throwout (release) bearing, activating the pressure plate.

clutch pressure plate - the part of a clutch assembly that is used to hold the driven disc against the flywheel. The pressure plate is composed of a cover and coil springs, driving disc and release levers, or a diaphragm spring.

clutch release bearing - a sealed ball or roller bearing unit that rides on a sleeve over the transmission input shaft, and acts on the pressure plate to disengage the clutch disc when the clutch release mechanism is applied. Also called a throwout bearing.

clutch throwout bearing - see **clutch release bearing.**

constant mesh - in a transmission, where all gears are constantly in contact and turning with one another.

constant velocity (CV) joint - a flexible coupling between two shafts that allows each shaft to maintain the same speed regardless of operating angle.

corrode - gradual loss from a metal surface from chemical action.

corrosion - the eating into or wearing away of a substance gradually by rusting or chemical action.

countergear - a set of different size gears incorporated in one casting, used in a manual transmission.

crossmember - part of the vehicle frame structure, arranged transversely and attached to the frame rails at each side of the vehicle. Can be removable or welded in place.

CV-joint - see **constant velocity joint.**

--d--

dial indicator - a measuring device equipped with a readout dial used most often to determine end motion or irregularities.

diaphragm - flexible, impermeable membrane on which pressure acts to produce mechanical movement; in automotive terminology, any disc-shaped device; can be as diverse as thin membranes that separate two chambers in a component, and large metal discs that activate clutch pressure plates.

differential - gear assembly that transmits power from the driveshaft to the wheels; allows the outside wheel to turn faster than the inside when cornering.

differential carrier - enclosure for the differential and ring and pinion gears. Can be removable or integral part of axle housing. Also called differential housing.

differential case - housing for the differential pinion gears and side gears. Mounting point for ring gear.

differential housing - see **differential carrier.**

differential pinion gears - gear that are meshed with the differential side gears and rotate on the differential pinion shaft inside the differential case.

differential pinion shaft - a shaft mounted inside the differential case, provides support and pivot for the differential pinion gears.

differential side gears - gears that are meshed with the pinion gears inside the differential case and splined to the axle shafts.

direct drive - downward gear engagement in which the input shaft and output shaft are locked together; the gearing in a drivetrain in which one turn of the crankshaft equals one turn of the wheels.

double cardan universal joint - two cardan universal joints connected by a yoke; also called a constant velocity (CV) joint.

double offset joint - a type of plunger CV-joint used on the inboard side of the interconnecting shaft.

dowel - a peg or pin which fits into corresponding holes used for holding two parts together or to locate two parts in a set position.

driveline - all of the parts connecting the engine to the drive axle.

driveline angle - see **driveshaft angle.**

driveshaft - transfers power from the transmission to the differential on a rear-wheel drive vehicle. Consists of a hollow metal tube with universal joints at each end, each of which is attached to yokes at the transmission and differential.

driveshaft angle - the installation angle of the driveshaft off the true horizontal; also called driveline angle.

drivetrain - all of the components that generate power and transfer it to the vehicle's wheels.

--e--

end clearance - the built-in extent of movement of a component, usually fore-and-aft.

end-play - the amount of axial or end-to-end movement in a shaft due to clearance in the bearings; the regulated movement of a component, usually a shaft, during operation.

excessive wear - in mechanical terms, wear of a component that exceeds designed limits; wear caused by overloading a part that is in an out-of-balance condition, resulting in lower-than-normal life expectancy of the part being subjected to the adverse operating condition.

extension housing - aluminum or cast iron enclosure for the transmission output shaft and bearings, speedometer drive and driven gears. Provides support for driveshaft slip yoke.

--f--

fatigue - deterioration of a bearing metal under excessive intermittent loads or prolonged operation; in mechanical terms, the tendency of a material, especially metal, to fail under repeated applications of stress.

feeler gauge - thin metal strip manufactured in precise thickness and used to measure clearance between parts; usually part of a set.

ferrous - containing or derived from iron.

ferrous metal - metal that contains iron or steel and is subject to rust.

flange - a projecting rim or collar on a component used for holding it in place, giving it strength or guiding it into place or attaching it; a part mounted on the pinion gear that provides the mounting point for the rear universal joint of the driveshaft.

flywheel - a cast iron or steel wheel mounted to the end of the crankshaft; helps to smooth the engine's power delivery, the teeth around its circumference provide an engagement for the starter, and it provides the mounting points for the pressure plate and friction surface for the clutch disc.

foot pound - a unit of measurement for torque. One foot pound is the torque obtained by a force of one pound applied to a wrench handle that is 12-in. long; a unit of energy required to raise a weight of one pound, a distance of one foot.

force - a pushing effort measured in pounds; the form of energy that puts an object at rest into motion or changes the motion of a moving object.

forge - to shape metal; to stamp into a desired shape through mechanical means, after heating.

forging - the process of shaping metal by stamping it into a desired shape.

four-wheel drive (4WD) - system that supplies power to both the front and rear wheels of the vehicle when activated.

free-play - the measurable travel in a mechanical device between the time force is applied and work is accomplished; looseness in a linkage between the start of application and the actual movement of the device, such as the movement in the steering wheel before the wheels start to turn.

free travel - distance a clutch pedal moves before it begins to take up slack in the clutch linkage; essentially the same as free-play, usually applied to shaft movement.

freewheel - a mechanical device that engages the driving member to impart motion to a driven member in one direction but not the other; in automotive terms, a device that permits the driveshaft to continue turning when its speed exceeds that of the crankshaft, thus allowing free coasting with the gear train engaged.

friction - the resistance to the motion of two moving objects in contact with each other.

front-wheel drive (FWD) - the entire drivetrain is located at the front of and drives the front wheels of the vehicle.

full floating axle - system where the weight of the vehicle is supported by the axle housing and the axle bearing is located outside of the axle housing; most often used on trucks.

fully synchronized - in a manual transmission, where gears are changed using synchronizers.

--g--

galling - weld-like damage to a metal due to lack of lubrication.

Glossary of Terms

gasket - a material such as artificial rubber, cork, or steel used to seal between parts that would otherwise leak fuel, coolant, lubricants or combustion gases.

gear - a toothed wheel, disc, etc. designed to mesh with another or with the thread of a worm; used to transfer or change motion.

gear pitch - number of teeth per given unit of pitch diameter. Gear pitch is determined by dividing the number of teeth by the pitch diameter of the gear.

gear ratio - the number of revolutions a driving gear must turn to rotate the driven gear through one revolution. Numerical value determined by dividing the number of teeth on the driven gear by the number of teeth on the driving gear; the ratio between the number of teeth on meshing gears.

gear reduction - when a smaller gear drives a larger gear, there is a speed reduction but an increase in torque.

go/no-go gauge - a measuring tool that tells if a tolerance is met or not.

grind - to machine a surface with an abrasive wheel.

--h--

halfshaft - transfers power from the transaxle to the front wheels on a front-wheel drive vehicle. Also used on some vehicles with rear-wheel drive and independent rear suspension to transfer power from the differential to the rear wheels. Consists of a stub shaft that is splined into the differential side gear, another stub shaft that is splined into the wheel hub, an interconnecting shaft, and two CV-joints, which connect the interconnecting shaft to the stub shafts.

hard spot - an area in a casting which has become harder (more dense) than the surrounding material; areas in the friction surface of a brake drum or rotor that have become harder than the surrounding metal.

heel - the outside or larger part of a gear tooth; the bottom of the cam lobe's base circle.

helical gear - a gear in which the teeth are cut so as to form a spiral; gear with teeth that are cut at an angle or are spiral to the gear's axis of rotation.

heli-coil - one type of thread repair device that consists of a spring loaded stainless steel coil.

hub - mounting point for the wheel on an axle or spindle; the part of the synchronizer assembly that is splined to the transmission shaft; the center part of a wheel, gear, etc., that rides on a shaft.

hunting gearset - differential gearset where any one pinion gear tooth contacts all ring gear teeth.

hydraulic clutch - a clutch that is engaged by hydraulic pressure.

hydraulic pressure - pressure exerted through a liquid.

hypoid gear - a bevel-cut gear in a system in which the driven gear is not in the same plane as the drive gear. A type of spiral, beveled ring and pinion gearset in a differential. Hypoid gears mesh below the ring gear centerline.

--i--

ID - inside diameter.

inch pound - one twelfth of a foot pound.

inner bearing race - inner part of a ball or roller bearing that provides a surface for the balls or rollers to rotate.

input shaft - the shaft that is splined to the clutch disc and transfers power from the engine into the transmission; the shaft to which torque is applied, usually carrying the drive gear or gears.

insert - a part of the synchronizer assembly that fits between the hub and sleeve, also called key or plate. The insert spring pushes the inserts into the sleeve, helping to center the sleeve on the hub.

insert spring - exerts pressure on the inserts in a synchronizer assembly.

integral - made up of parts forming a whole.

--l--

lash - the amount of clearance between components in a geartrain or valvetrain.

limited slip differential - a type of differential that uses clutches to supply a major portion of the drive torque to the wheel that has better traction when one wheel is slipping.

live axle - an axle on which the wheels are firmly affixed, with the axle driving the wheels.

lubrication - the process of introducing a friction reducing substance between moving parts to reduce wear.

--m--

master cylinder - the primary fluid pressurizing device in some hydraulic systems. In automotive use, it is found in the brake and hydraulic clutch systems and is pedal-activated, either directly or through a vacuum assist unit.

mesh - to fit closely together or interlock, as the fit of gear teeth.

micrometer - a precision measuring instrument. When a micrometer measures in thousandths of an inch, one turn of its thimble results in 0.025-in. movement of its spindle. There are 40 threads per inch ($1/40$th inch = 0.025-in.)

--n--

needle bearing - an anti-friction device that consists of a number (usually a large number) of thin rollers riding within races.

nonhunting gearset - differential gearset in which one drive pinion gear tooth contacts only three ring gear teeth after several rotations.

normal wear - the average expected wear when operating under normal conditions.

--o--

OD - outside diameter.

out-of-round - when a previously round hole or bore has different diameters when measured at different points due to wear or distortion.

outer bearing race - outer part of a ball or roller bearing that provides a surface for the balls or rollers to rotate. Can be integral with the bearing or a separate part.

output shaft - the shaft that delivers the power that has come through the transmission or transaxle.

overdrive - a gear assembly that outputs more shaft revolutions than were input.

--p--

pilot bearing - a needle roller bearing, installed in the end of the crankshaft or center of the flywheel, that supports the end of the transmission input shaft.

pilot bushing - a plain bearing, installed in the end of the crankshaft or center of the flywheel, that supports the end of the transmission input shaft.

pilot journal - a mechanical journal that slides inside the pilot bearing or bushing and guides its movement.

pinion - the smaller of two meshing gears.

pinion gear - the smaller, drive gear of the ring and pinion gearset; one of the gears inside the differential that rotates on the differential pinion shaft; rotates around the sun gear in a planetary gearset.

pitch - in machinery, the distance between corresponding points on two adjacent gear teeth, or threads of a screw or bolt measured along the axis; the angle of the valve spring twist. A variable pitch valve spring has unevenly-spaced coils.

pitting - surface irregularities caused by corrosion or excess wear.

play - the relative movement between or among parts.

plunger joint - the inboard CV-joint on a halfshaft, so called because the joint moves in and out in response to the suspension's up-and-down movement, which causes the distance between the transaxle and the wheel to change. The movement takes place within the joint, with the tripod rollers or double offset ball bearings moving in and out on elongated grooves in the yoke or outer race.

preload - tightening a bearing a specified amount past zero lash to eliminate axial play.

press fit - when a part is slightly larger than a hole it must be forced together with a press.

pressure plate - the driving member of the clutch assembly. Coil springs or a diaphragm spring in the pressure plate exert pressure on the clutch disc, holding it against the flywheel.

--r--

race - a channel in the inner or outer ring of an anti-friction bearing in which the balls or rollers operate.

rear-wheel drive (RWD) - system where the driveline drives the rear wheels of the vehicle. Most often the engine is located in the front of the vehicle and a transmission and driveshaft connect to a drive axle, however there are also systems where the entire driveline is located toward the rear of the vehicle.

release bearing - see **clutch release bearing**.

reverse idler gear - a gear used to reverse the direction of power in a transmission.

Glossary of Terms

ring gear - the larger, driven gear of the ring and pinion gearset; the largest member in a planetary gearset, also known as the internal gear or annulus. The internal teeth of the gear mesh with and rotate on the planetary pinions.

roller bearing - an anti-friction device made up of hardened inner and outer races between which steel rollers move.

runout - wobble or deflection beyond a rotating part's normal plane of movement.

Rzeppa joint - a type of fixed ball-type CV-joint consisting of a star shaped inner race, which is splined to the interconnecting shaft of the halfshaft, six balls, a cage, an outer race, which is usually part of the stub shaft, and a boot.

--s--

score - a scratch, ridge or groove on a finished surface; to mar a surface in that way.

seal - a part, usually made of rubber or plastic, installed around a moving part or shaft to prevent leaks.

self-adjusting clutch - a clutch linkage system, usually a cable, where a ratcheting mechanism automatically adjusts clutch pedal play.

semi-floating axle - system where the axle bearing is located inside the axle housing and the weight of the vehicle is supported by the axle.

shift fork - a device in a manual transmission that moves the synchronizer assembly sleeve, in response to movement from the shift linkage.

shift rails - the parts of transmission shift linkage that transfer motion from the driver-controlled gear shift lever to the shift forks.

shifter - the lever operated by the driver to shift the transmission. The shifter is attached directly to internal linkage in the transmission or it is mounted on the outside of the transmission or on the frame or vehicle floor, and connected to the transmission or transaxle by external linkage rods or cables.

shim - thin sheets of material, usually metal, used as spacers to control the distance between parts.

slave cylinder - a device that is connected to the release bearing in a hydraulic clutch system. When the clutch pedal is depressed, hydraulic fluid flows from the master cylinder through the hydraulic fluid line to the slave cylinder. Pressure in the system causes the slave cylinder to act on the release bearing, disengaging the clutch.

sleeve - a thin metal liner, such as is commonly used in a cylinder bore; the outer part of the synchronizer assembly. When shifting gears, the sleeve moves along the splined inner hub in response to the shift fork, forcing the blocking ring against the gear cone and then, when the gear is at the same speed, slides over the blocking ring and gear engagement teeth, locking the gear to the synchronizer hub and shaft.

slip yoke - a driveline component that is splined to the transmission output shaft and connected to the driveshaft front U-joint. Allows in and out movement on the transmission extension housing in response to rear suspension movement.

splines - grooves cut into the outside or inside surface of a component to enable it to fit with another component having corresponding grooves. Commonly used to keep a component secured on a rotating shaft.

sponginess - the feel of a soft or mushy brake pedal usually caused by trapped air in the hydraulic system.

straightedge - a long, flat steel strip with perfectly straight edges, used for checking surfaces for warpage.

synchronizer - a type of clutch assembly used in a manual transmission to shift gears. Consists of a hub splined to the main shaft, inserts (keys) and insert springs, outer sleeve and blocking rings. There are grooves machined into the sleeves to capture the shift forks, which transfer the motion from the gearshift linkage. The sleeve moves along the splined inner hub in response to the shift fork, forcing the blocking ring against the gear cone and then, when the gear is at the same speed, slides over the blocking ring and gear engagement teeth, locking the gear to the synchronizer hub and shaft.

--t--

throwout bearing - see **clutch release bearing.**

thrust - the continuous pressure of one object against another.

thrust load - load placed on a part that is parallel to the center of the axis.

thrust washer - a metal or plastic device that separates rotating parts from each other and non-rotating parts, and absorbs thrust loads; used to take up end thrust and prevent excessive end-play.

tolerance - the difference between the allowable maximum and minimum dimensions of a mechanical part; the basis for determining the accuracy of a fitting.

torque - twisting effort on a shaft or bolt.

transaxle - a unit that houses the transmission and differential assembly. Most often used in front wheel drive vehicles.

transfer case - attached to or connected to the transmission in a four-wheel drive vehicle. Transfers power to both front and rear axles.

transmission - transfers the engine's power to the driveshaft and the rear wheels. Contains a series of gears that provide torque multiplication, so the vehicle can be moved from a standstill and also cruise at highway speeds at lower engine rpms.

transverse - perpendicular or at a right angle to a front-to-back centerline.

tripod joint - a type of CV-joint consisting of a spider, which is splined to the interconnecting shaft of the halfshaft, three rollers that turn on needle roller bearings located between the spider and rollers, a housing, or yoke, that is part of the stub shaft, and a boot.

--*u*--

U-joint - see **universal joint.**

universal joint (U-joint) - a joint that allows the driveshaft to transmit torque at different angles as the suspension moves up and down.

--*w*--

warpage - a condition that exists when a part is bent or twisted; the degree to which a part deviates from flatness.

--*y*--

yoke - the mounting points for the U-joints. Attached to or part of a tube or flange.

NOTES